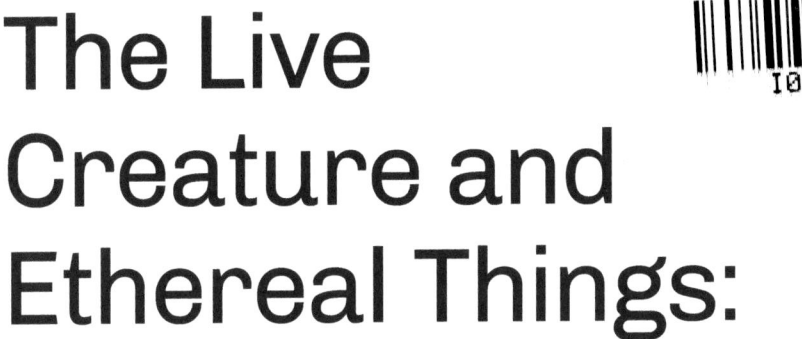

The Live Creature and Ethereal Things:

Physics in Culture

Edited by Fiona Crisp & Nicola Triscott

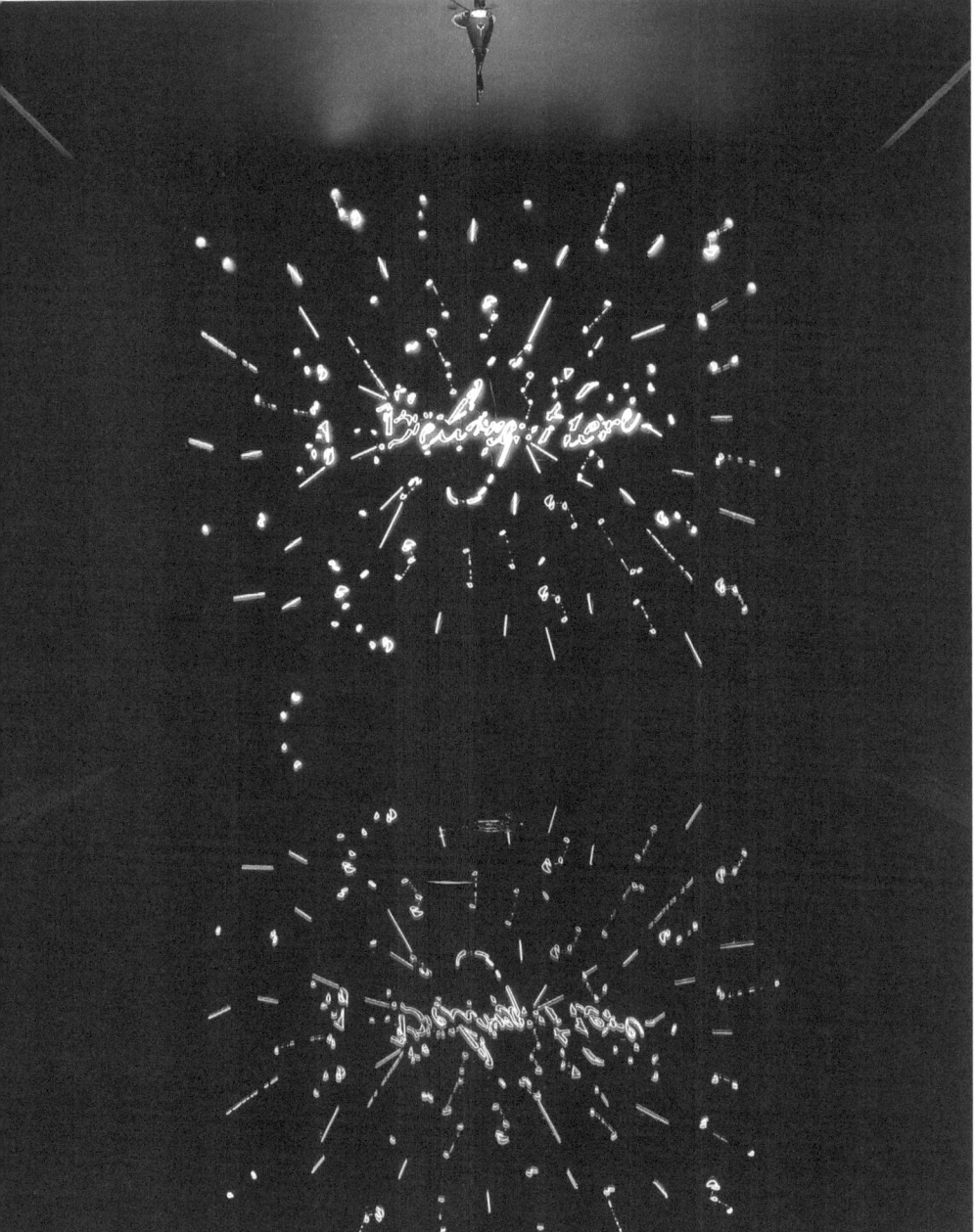

Contents

Foreword

Given that the laws of physics govern the way our universe operates and therefore permeate every aspect of our lives, I've often found it unfortunate how the subject of physics is distanced from other aspects of what we might broadly describe as our culture. Physics is an incredibly creative endeavour - it expands our minds and is constantly asking questions about what is, and what is possible. It provides us with fascinating artefacts in the form of new technologies and tools, while simultaneously firing the imagination. But because the culture of physics itself is weighed down by stereotypes and jargon, combined with the fact that it often deals with the intangible and abstract, it means that for all too many people it remains distant and unrelatable.

As is shown in this collection of essays, the sophistication of the discourse between physicists and artists is increasing and enduring, long-term collaborations are developing. We are moving from a world in which artists are merely 'inspired by' physics to them actively using it and grappling with it in the development of their work. While physicists aren't just becoming better at communicating their science, but are also expanding their thinking about their research and employing new methodologies. Thus, I find *The Live Creature and Ethereal Things* a welcome contribution to the discourse between physics and the arts. The contributors to this collection each make vital points about the culture of physics, the place of physics in our culture, and the interface and interplay between physics and the arts.

Johanna Kieniewicz, Institute of Physics, 2018

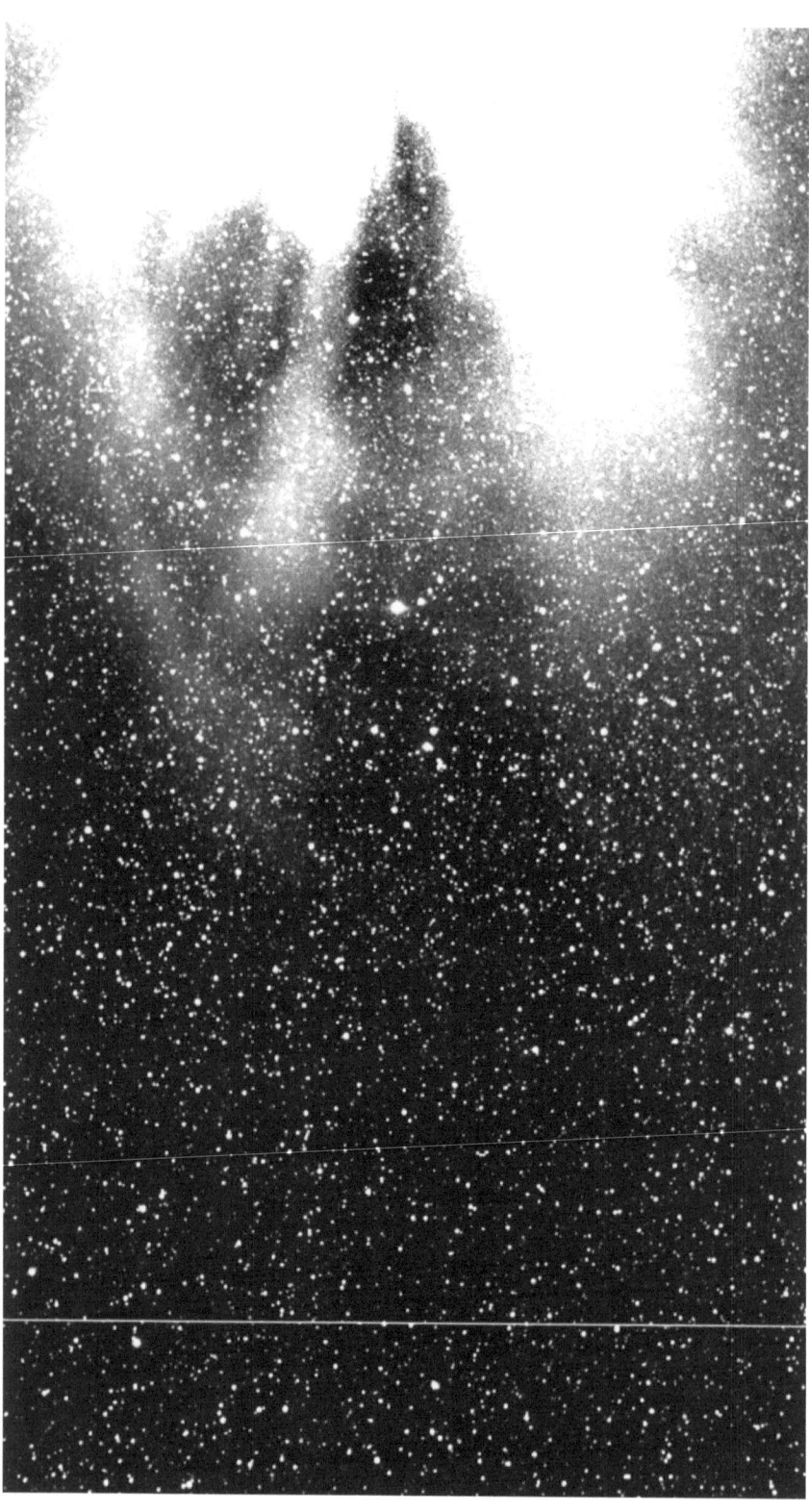

Semiconductor, *Black Rain*, 2009
Single channel and installation

Introduction
— Fiona Crisp & Nicola Triscott

"The Sun, the Moon, the Earth and its contents are material to form greater things, that is, ethereal things - greater things than the Creator himself has made" — John Keats, 1817

The Live Creature and Ethereal Things: Physics in Culture has emerged from an ongoing research project led by artist Fiona Crisp and curator Nicola Triscott, addressing the question of how to bring fundamental physics into the human experience – how to understand and make big science "intimate", to use the phrase of astronomer Roger Malina – and the role that contemporary art might play in this.

Many areas of contemporary science, including cosmology, particle physics and astrophysics, operate at scales and levels of complexity that lie beyond the imaginative and cognitive grasp of lay publics. Today, with advanced science and technology and the accelerating impact of human activity on the planet, we live in new scales of size and speed that we cannot easily assimilate. If so much knowledge comes through scientific instruments and abstract mathematics, how can we humans - biological sensing beings that the philosopher John Dewey refers to as the "live creative" - make sense of it within our own experience? This isn't just an academic concern. It impacts deeply on the practice of physics, from the backgrounds of those who are attracted to study physics and then remain within the profession, to how physics is understood and valued by the public, and the broader cultural imaginary of science.

As part of our research, we convened a workshop in October 2017, in partnership with the Institute of Physics in London. *The Live Creature and Ethereal Things* brought together a group of contemporary artists, curators and physicists to explore different aspects of these questions. While our original vision of the workshop was to re-imagine the non-expert's encounter with fundamental physics and the physics of the universe, the workshop went far deeper than this, exploring the role of personality, power and culture in physics, presenting physics as a material and human practice, and examining philosophical notions of fundamental physics as emergent (a state of "dynamic happening") rather than elemental. Worshop participants discussed the value of cross-pollination between the practices of art and physics and how this can happen in a non-instrumalising way. Through the workshop two distinct but intimately connected themes began to emerge: namely 'The Culture of Physics' and 'Physics in Culture'.

This book seeks to reflect some of these discussions and ideas and to share them with a broader constituency. We have invited several physicists and contemporary artists, workshop participants and others, to share with us their reflections on our overarching questions. We have asked them to make these reflections personal to their own interests, personalities and practices. For many contributors – both artists and scientists – such reflections have taken visual as well as textual form.

This inquiry has been triggered by Fiona Crisp's Research
Fellowship, *Material Sight*, that has been generously supported
by the Leverhulme Trust and hosted by Arts Catalyst. *Material
Sight* employs non-documentary photography and film to bring
science back within our world as experience, using still and moving
imagery to place us in a bodily relation to the physical spaces
and laboratories where fundamental science is performed. The
project has evolved into a co-inquiry between Crisp, Nicola Triscott
(Artistic Director of Arts Catalyst), and an evolving network of
artists, curators, physicists and other thinkers.

10

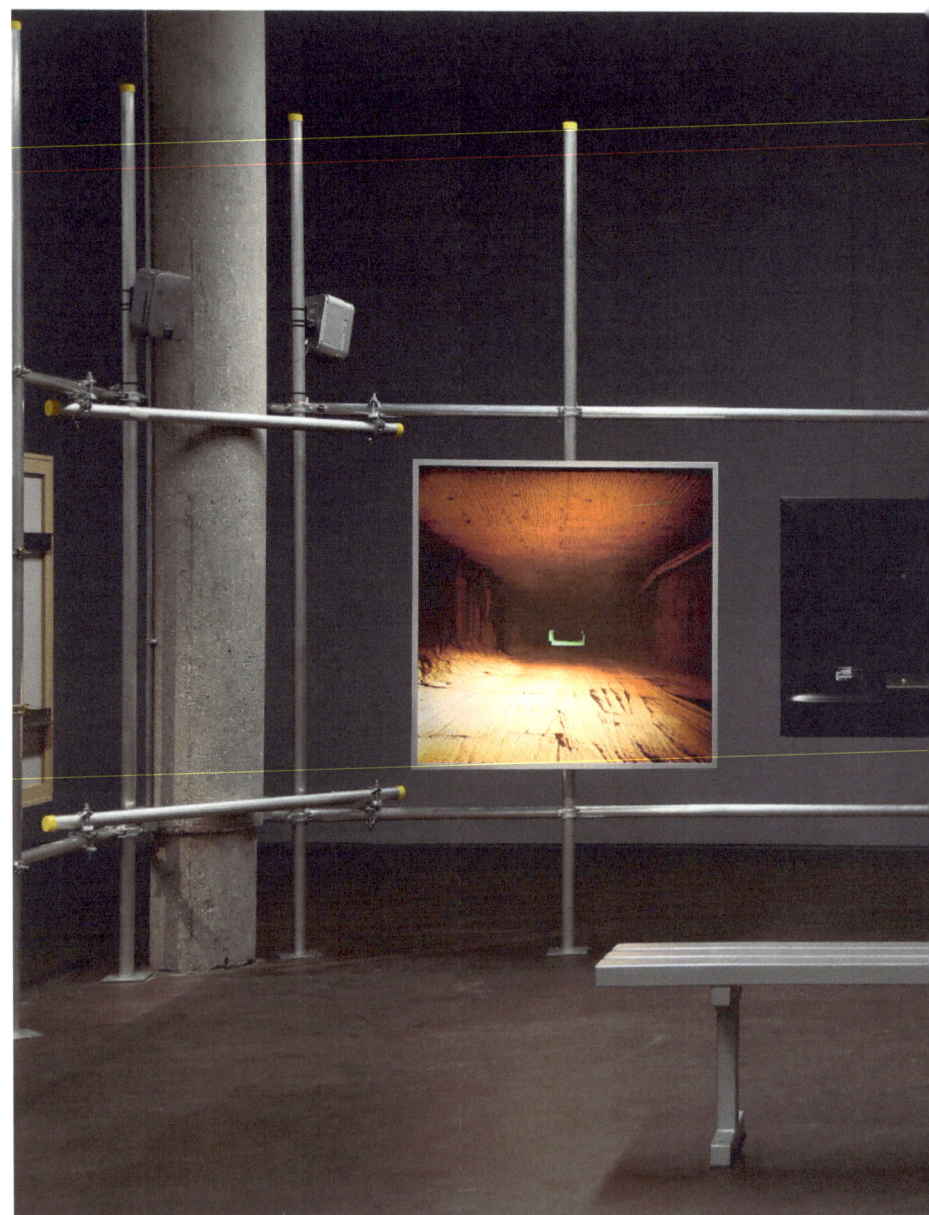

Fiona Crisp, *Material Sight* (detail), 2018
Northern Gallery for Contemporary Art
Image courtesy the artist and Matt's Gallery, London

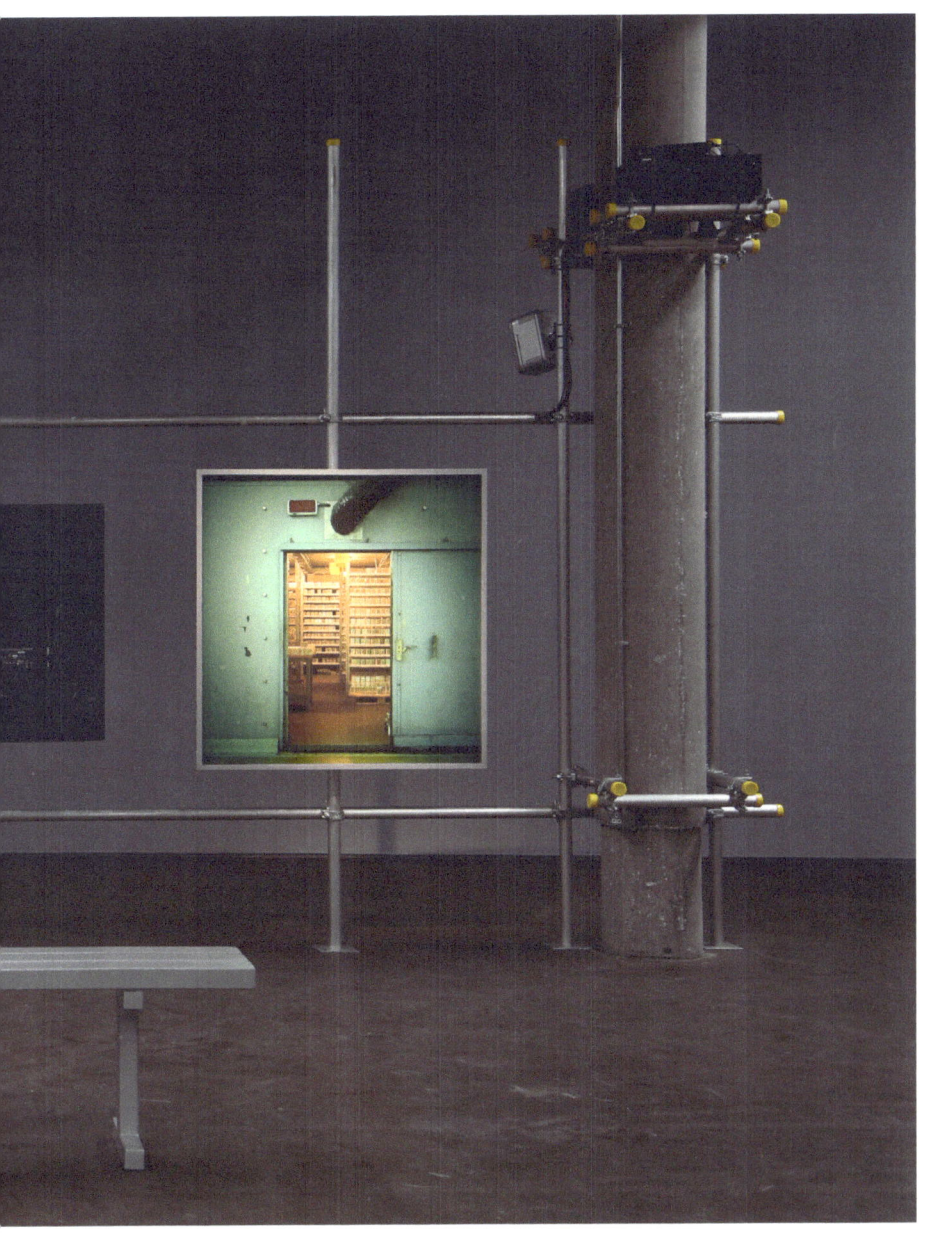

The Live Creature & Ethereal Things
— Nicola Triscott

When the philosopher John Dewey wrote about *Art as Experience* in 1934,[1] he was attempting to shift the understanding of what is important and characteristic about art from its physical manifestations in the object to the process in its entirety, a process in which the fundamental element is no longer the material "work of art" but rather the development of "an experience", such an experience being something that personally affects your life. He used the term "ethereal things", which he took from Keats, to condemn aesthetic theories that elevated art too far above its pragmatic experiential roots. In a similar spirit to Dewey's critique of art theory in the 1930s, I want to broaden the framing of contemporary physics from a methodology and field of knowledge to a process; an exchange between the material and the "live creature", the human, and a practical, experienced reality.

Astrophysics and particle physics probe the limits of the known, the limits of language and concept, and present a kind of abstraction or transcendence that can free us from commonsensical thinking. Yet they are undertaken by human beings in real world laboratories and observatories, driven, shaped and influenced by those people's cultural backgrounds, education, funding requirements, teaching obligations, family commitments, societal norms, aspirations, rivalries and dreams. How do these human beings co-create knowledge about the structure and mechanics of the universe, and how is this process and knowledge put forth into the world?

These questions are intertwined because the way in which physics represents itself to the non-expert tends to focus on facts and knowledge, rather than the ways and whys and wherefores by which it is produced. This can lead to a gap in the cultural imaginary and social understanding of physics, a gap between an awareness of these people called physicists and this set of knowledge called physics, in which there is little sense of how physics unfolds through its processes, personalities, and places, and how one thing leads to or affects the other. Within this gap, as Pugh and Girod similarly note of science education that focuses solely on understanding scientific concepts, we can also lose awareness that science has the potential "to enrich everyday life, vitalise experience, and provide us with aesthetic satisfaction".[2]

Given current concerns around science recruitment and public belief in and support for science, it is timely to address this gap. In this essay, I will approach the subject of bringing the physics into the human experience - or bringing the human back to the centre of physics - from two angles, one a discussion of the culture

1   John Dewey, *Art as Experience* (New York: Minton, Balch & Company, 1934).
2   Kevin J. Pugh and Mark Girod. "Science, Art, and Experience: Constructing a Science Pedagogy From Dewey's Aesthetics, *Journal of Science Teacher Education* 18, no.1 (2007): 9–27. http://www.jstor.org/stable/43156404.

of physics, questioning the notion of a 'no culture' of physics, the other a consideration of the expression of physics as a human, material activity into wider society. These two perspectives broadly parallel those of the artist and physicist contributors to this book. In addition, I will interweave some thoughts on the value of artistic practice to physics itself and the wider cultural expression and societal role of physics.

The culture of physics

To posit the existence of a "culture of physics", and to suggest that culture might shape how physics is done, can trigger polarised positions. There are those who think that the social environment, belief systems and behaviours of the physics community must influence what science is pursued and how, while others insist that the endeavour of physics is not affected by its culture, or that it is culture-free.[3] The so-called "science wars"[4] are a sad example of binary position taking, in which scientific realists clashed with postmodernists, whom they regarded as rejecting scientific objectivity, the scientific method and scientific knowledge.

This is a great shame, because recognising and enabling studies of the culture of physics could potentially shed light on some of the issues that concern scientists, those around the recruitment, retention, and diversity of scientists, and those concerning public support for science. In addition, enabling further porosity with other cultural influences and disciplinary perspectives could potentially bring benefits to science itself, in terms of alternative perspectives and methodologies and new ideas, which seem entirely in tune with science's pursuit of inquiry into how the universe works. The position of some scientists that nothing cultural (and certainly nothing artistic) could possibly affect the scientific method seems unlikely, given that it is humans who create and re-create the scientific method. There is no one immutable method, and the scientific method tends to evade simple definition, although there are principles in common around testing and replicability.

Many sociological and anthropological studies have shown that physics is a culture with internal beliefs and value systems, and that there are differences in cultures of science across different parts of the world, reflecting varied histories, societal attitudes, institutional contexts, and dominant social make up. Yet, many scientists still prefer to believe their world is basically independent

3   Broadly, when I use the term "culture", I am referring to the customary beliefs, social forms, and material traits of a particular social group, so when I refer to a culture of physics, I am speaking of the dominant characteristics, beliefs, social behaviours, and traditions of the physics community. When I refer to wider culture, I am talking about the social norms, customs and behaviours of the society within which physics is situated, which transform over time.

4   The science wars were a series of intellectual exchanges during the 1990s, primarily in the USA, between scientific realists and postmodernist critics. The scientific realists argued that scientific knowledge is real, and accused the postmodernists of having effectively rejected the scientific method and scientific knowledge, while the postmodernists argued that scientific theories are social constructs.

of culture, "a culture of no culture", as anthropologist Sharon Traweek terms it, "which longs passionately for a world without loose ends, without temperament, gender, nationalism or other sources of disorder."[5]

Despite this longing (or ideal), gender and cultural background do seem to matter in the self-selection, institutional selection, and retention of those who enter into the culture of physics. In Cathrine Hasse's analysis of connections between gender and physics,[6] she notes that, in general, the natural sciences report increasing problems with recruitment, especially of female physics students. Notably, she finds that this is primarily in the North-Western world, where there is also a disproportionate leakage of women from scientific careers at every stage in the academic hierarchy, which challenges the notion of an internally self-regulating culture-free science. Attempts to explain this away in terms of restrictions in educational or employment opportunities for women in the wider culture or childcare responsibilities are belied by puzzling differential patterns, where the proportion of female physicists is found to be higher the further South and East we go, not just in Europe but across the globe. In her fascinating study, in which she interviewed physicists from different European countries, Hasse found a connection to physics that had nothing to do with gender (indeed the Italian female physics students did not regard physics as a 'gendered' subject at all) but rather concerned the relationship between humanities and natural sciences in a local, cultural-historically shaped context. It was this cultural contrast that gave Hasse new insight into the gender differences found. In Italy, she discovered, it was possible to study physics at university level with a background in the humanities: "… many of the very successful Italian professors in physics that I interviewed turned out to have entered their study with a high school background as classical studies. They were versed in philosophy and cultural history, studying Aristotle in Greek, reading Cicero in Latin and the like",[7] whereas in Denmark, as in the UK, humanities and natural sciences are generally seen as mutually exclusive. Indeed, a background in classical studies was seen as an asset to a physicist. Hasse reports one professor in Italy, coming to physics from a scientific background, explaining:

> I myself have a background equivalent to a mathematical-physicist high school student in Denmark. But here in Italy it is rather an advantage to have a classical linguistic background, when you start physics studies at university level. The 'classical' students are simply better at analyzing. What we learned in science high school was to think much more 'mechanically' –

5   Sharon Traweek, *Beamtimes and Lifetimes* (Boston MA.: Harvard University Press, 1988): 162.
6   Cathrine Hasse, "Cultural Models of Physics: An Analysis of Historical Connections Between Hard Sciences, Humanities and Gender in Physics", in *University Science and Mathematics Education in Transition*, eds. Ole Skovsmose, Paola Valero and Ole Ravn Christensen. (Boston, MA.: Springer, 2009).
7   Ibid., 14.

to think in the correct answers. I have always believed students with a classical background are the most advantaged.[8]

Further, Hasse notes, her interviews with Danish, Swedish and English female physicists showed a much more problematic relationship between being female and being a physicist than with the Italians. Many reported that through their whole career they had "felt like outsiders".[9] In these North Western European cultures, she remarks, people have come to understand a connection between physics and "hard science", and to connect hard science with being male. These connections are not made when you move South and East.

This suggests that not only does gender matter in the selection of those who pass into physics, but so do personality traits and cultural and creative interests. In this volume, physicist Suchitra Sebastian makes a similar point:

> People in the field assume that to be a good physicist you have to be "like them". I think in their mind they're not selecting for anything other than good physics, but of course in reality they're selecting for a plethora of characteristics that are to do with the person and not just the physics that they do.

Sebastian did her undergraduate degree in physics at a liberal arts college and says that her multidisciplinary outlook conflicted with what was expected of her when she became a physicist. She felt huge pressure to be "a certain kind of physicist", to have gravitas and to be interested only in physics, and therefore she separated out the parts of her personality that didn't fit. It was only when she began to engage with the public that she realised they simply weren't interested in hearing about the science she was doing when she spoke about it in the abstract. They sensed she wasn't being authentic, and it was then that she began to reconnect her other interests with her science.

All the physicists who have contributed to this book, which follows a workshop that I convened with Fiona Crisp at the Institute of Physics, were asked to bring their individual authentic selves to their writing and to write about science in a way that only they could. This has produced several insightful and compelling contributions that weave connections between their scientific selves and their cultural selves and other interests. Tara Shears expresses a personality trait that perhaps makes her an easier "fit" for the way the physics world is at the moment: a joy in simplicity and in finding a way to order the world. She notes that "particle physics is full of people like me". She writes of her love of mathematics, but also of her love for literature, poetry and art,to which she feels drawn for their economy and power of expression, as much as that of mathematics. Flaviu Cipcigan meanwhile directly relates his passion for dance to physics, while Mark Neyrinck

8 Ibid., 15
9 Ibid.

discusses his fascination for origami as a way to explore cosmic structure, and Marek Kukula reflects on a history of art that has powered new perspectives about science and its relation to disruptive thinking, a characteristic that, he suggests, the paradigm-breaking astronomer Galileo inherited from his father, the musician and composer Vincent Galilei.

Physicist Chamkaur Ghag and artist Ansuman Biswas discuss embodied knowledge in their conversation, which starts from a shared interest in meditation - a "contemplative science". They critique the culture of "nonstop thinking" in physics, noting that "the speed at which things are progressing is an indication that there's very little reflection". Ghag calls for scientists to slow down, come out of their heads, and ask themselves where science is going. He suggests that the next evolution of the scientific method requires putting science back into context, and considers that such an approach would be welcomed by many scientists, although the established culture and structures of physics make this challenging.

I sense that Ghag and Biswas' conversation represents an emerging new mode of science, in which the skills and interests of people inside and outside science are starting to come together to create new ways for people to engage with science and for scientists to develop a new ethical relationship with the world.

Physics in culture

Having outlined some of the arguments for recognising that physics is a human experience, with its own culture, and how this recognition can benefit the physics community, in this section, I will explore some of the urgencies for physics to connect to wider culture and society, and how approaches and insights from artistic practice are helping to create these new connections as well as contributing to science itself.

Astronomer Roger Malina in this volume remarks that one of the problems for modern science is that it doesn't make sense on the human scale. Almost all physical knowledge about the world and the universe now comes through scientific instruments and is pursued at scales and distances far beyond our human sensing. In fact, he adds, much science is done today by experiments on data rather than experiments on the world. As more and more science comes to us through this mediated data, there are cultural implications in the disconnect between the science and the intimate world that we live in every day. This disconnect is a problem because it is important to be able to know which scientific facts are useful and which are not useful, and this requires that scientific knowledge is assimilated by society and contextualised.[10] He refers to this process as "making science intimate". While scientists do this, for example, creating simulations that mimic how the world works, he considers that artists increasingly play an invaluable

---

10 Roger Malina, "Intimate Science; Or Artists in the Dark Universe", a talk given at Sonic Acts (2010), https://vimeo.com/12920830.

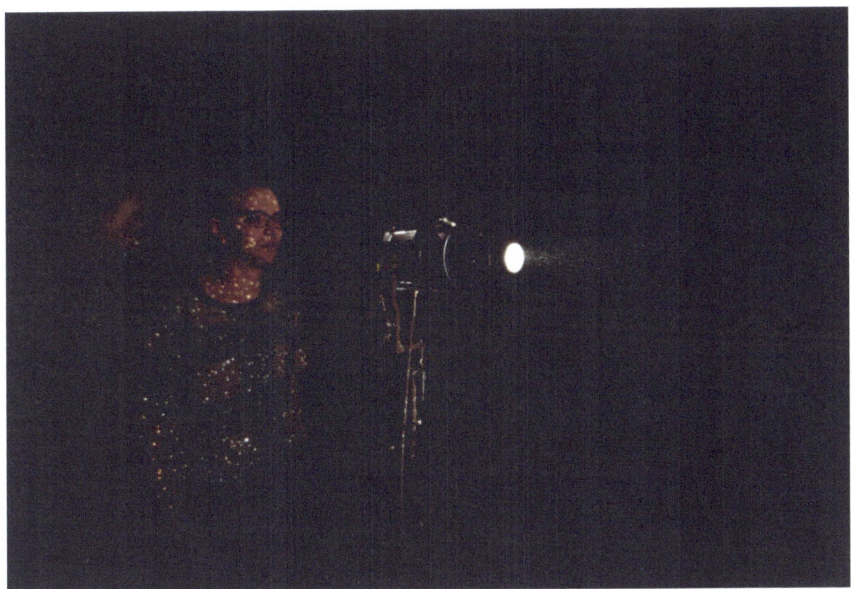

role in this process, as do movements such as citizen science and people's science. Bringing artists into the scientific realm, he argues, can lead to better science, and can also lead to different science through the process of embedding science into wider society.

The contribution that artists can make to science is increasingly recognised by scientific institutions, both in terms of what artists bring to science itself and the scientific environment, and to developing a more fluid relationship between science and society. More and more science institutions are setting up schemes designed to bring artists into the realm of science, not as illustrators but to bring their different perspectives and practices to work alongside and inform those of science. Perhaps the most long-standing of these is the MIT (Massachusetts Institute of Technology) Visiting Artists programme. Another well-known example is Arts@CERN, the official arts programme of CERN, the large particle physics research facility in Switzerland, which CERN's Head of Arts Mónica Bello discusses in this volume.

One of MIT's artists in residence was Tomás Saraceno. An artist trained as an architect, Saraceno deploys insights from engineering, physics, chemistry, aeronautics and materials science in his work. During his MIT residency, the artist investigated the intricate geometry of spider webs and developed an original method to scan a three-dimensional web. Learning that spiders are known to use many astronomical cues for navigation, including the position of the moon and patterns formed by polarisation of light in the sky, Saraceno was inspired to produce a series of works, in collaboration with arachnologists, astrophysicists, architects

Tomás Saraceno, *Hyperweb of the Present*, 2017
Courtesy the artist and galleries — see p.58
Photography © see pictures

and engineers, involving live spiders spinning universes. In these spiderweb-universes, intricate filaments allude to dwarf and spiral galaxies, nebulae and quasars. His largest work, *How to Entangle the Universe in a Spider Web*, involved 7000 spiders in its creation. In this volume, cosmologist Mark Neyrinck remarks on the compelling correspondences between spiderwebs and the cosmic "web" that give a rigorous underpinning to Saraceno's insight.

Artist group Semiconductor (Ruth Jarman and Joe Gerhardt) have undertaken many residencies in scientific institutions around the world, including at CERN. Their film *Do You Think Science*, made during a residency at NASA Space Sciences Laboratory in California, asks several space physicists an unheard question about the limits of scientific understanding, prompting most to pause and then falter their way through unfamiliar metaphysical terrain. One just laughs: "Everything? No!", then asks in bafflement: "Do people actually say yes?". Other works by Semiconductor, such as *Brilliant Noise* and *Black Rain*, mine raw unprocessed scientific data to create mesmerising static-filled, jittery, black and white films of solar storms, creating a radically different aesthetic from the hyper-coloured, cleaned up images of cosmic objects, such as those created from Hubble telescope data, with which we are more familiar.

The scientific method is not a static thing, as Malina notes in his text. It continues to evolve, indeed it could be said to need a redesign with the development of sciences of complexity and artificial intelligence. The work of artists, such as Saraceno and Semiconductor and many others not in this book, who work in the terrain of science, can help to inform scientists' intuitions, vocabularies, and the way that they conceptualise and describe things, as science continues to move forward.

Alongside this wave of artists working in labs, scientists are adopting practices from outside the scientific method to bring new insights and ways of thinking into their research. Mark Neyrinck has been using origami to help him gain new understanding of cosmic structures, increasing knowledge in both directions, from science to origami, and from origami to science, and sharing this with students. Biswas and Ghag reflect that meditation practice could help to develop a more contemplative and potentially embodied science, while Flaviu Cipcigan observes that certain forms of dance are distinctive and effective forms of bodily knowledge, and wonders how science - currently limited to mental knowledge - would look like as an intimate, embodied knowledge.

Even by simply working in proximity to the artists who venture into their domains, scientists can gain from the exchange of ideas and approaches that emerge from these encounters. James Wells, the theoretical physicist who was the scientific partner for CERN's artist in residence Julius von Bismarck, talks about the value of having a lengthy exchange with an artist. He found that their rigorous processes were something that they had in common, but that an artist cares much more about the impact of their work on people, whereas "scientists don't generally think that way; they don't understand the impact that their work, and what they choose to do and how they do it, has on students and other scientists and the general science community".[11] One of the things he'd learned from von Bismarck was that "it pays to think quite a bit about the impact of one's work; all the way from the grand questions of 'is this right for humans to be doing?' to day-to-day things". He also valued having someone around who sees the world in a different way, whose influence could shake up accepted mindsets, noting that the artist starts from what they want to do, rather than what they can do: "they have no barriers to thinking about things".

Such processes of dialogue and exchange with artists can also allow scientists to gain confidence in understanding the 'performative', the process by which science comes into being through the scientists' acts of imaginative performance of their own scientific methodologies, and then in starting to articulate that. The workshop we organised and this publication have shown that some scientists are happy to open up in this way. This is not about a whole new way of working but giving a sort of 'permission' for them to place themselves – the whole person – in relationship to their science.

For artists who work with scientists and scientific ideas, theirs is not a process of representation or illustration or interpretation. They are rarely motivated by desire to educate or inform people about science but simply by their own fascinations. However, they play an important role in the process of cultural assimilation of science by society, of making science intimate. Some of the ways in which artists in this volume (most of whom attended the workshop) help to make fundamental science at the edge of knowledge and at the furthest reaches of scale both personal and intimate include the contribution by Nahum, an artist who uses hypnosis in his practice. In his experimental performance text, Nahum probes our potential to have a personal, intimate encounter with the elusive, ephemeral neutrino. Annie Carpenter then playfully attempts to model a black hole accretion disk (the material in orbit around the central body) using an electric fan and some dry ice.

Fiona Crisp takes a different approach in her project, *Material Sight*, exploring how we might approach the remoteness of fundamental physics by being put in a sensory relation to the "endeavour" of physics. To this end, her installations use non-documentary photography, moving image and sound to build a tangible sense of encounter with the laboratories and extreme environments where experimental and theoretical physics is performed. A focus on the unheeded material spaces and overlooked equipment of physics is also at the heart of Semiconductor's film *Magnetic Movie*, in which the artists' visualisations of usually invisible magnetic fields around equipment in a laboratory conveys a sense of these normally overlooked lumps of lab equipment as animate and almost sentient. Phil Coy, meanwhile, uses poetry and images to give a lyrically different perspective to the equipment that physicists use.

11 CERN, "Interview with James Wells (Collide@CERN) for Swiss Info" (2012), https://videos.cern.ch/record/1483712.

Blanca Pujals reflects on the architecture of physics on a geopolitical scale, exploring how elementary particle physics laboratories have become vast assemblages of people, materials, technologies and politics, mapping particle colliders, neutrino observatories and emissions from nuclear test sites and power plants to visualise relationships across the planet. Jol Thomson also starts from the laboratory – in this case his journey to Lake Baikal in Siberia, which is being partially transformed by the Russians into a vast neutrino telescope - but uses this experience as the starting point to reflect on the things that we think we know but know inaccurately, and the need for some radical unlearning and re-learning. Here, he echoes both Ghag and Malina's musings on the magnitude of what we don't know about the universe.

In his expanding, re-configuring collection of rocks, Harry Lawson ponders on different relationships between technology, geology, knowledge, and time, what of our culture and knowledge will be preserved, and what may disappear into dust. This is reminiscent of an Arthur C Clarke story about a machine that sent probes out to the ends of the universe, found the answer, and then realised that there was no one left to tell it to.[12]

Dewey believed that participating in art (he did not differentiate between fine art and popular art, or between its creation and reception) was an instance of a special type of experience that gives life meaning. Artistic activity enriches our lives by investing everyday actions and objects with new meaning and alters how we perceive the world:

> The function of art has always been to break through the crust of conventionalized and routine consciousness. Common things, a flower, a gleam of moonlight, the song of a bird, not things rare and remote, are means with which the deeper levels of life are touched so that they spring up as desire and thought. This process is art ... Artists have always been the real purveyors of news, for it is not the outward happening in itself which is new, but the kindling by it of emotion, perception and appreciation.[13]

From Dewey's transaction to Barad's intra-action

In 1949, Dewey introduced the term transaction as a philosophical way of understanding the human as an "organism-environment" and of human life as not separated into mind and the world outside it. His transactional perspective makes no radical separation between the subject and the object of knowledge. Knowing in this view is a co-operative, flexible and open process, and all human behaviours, even the most advanced forms of scientific inquiry, are processes of the whole organism in transaction with its environment.

Through the 1920s and 30s, physicists had struggled with the enigmas and apparent paradoxes presented by developments in

20

12 Ansuman Biswas relayed this story in his conversation with Chamkaur Ghag
13 John Dewey, *The Public and its Problems* (New York: H. Holt and Company, 1927).

theoretical physics,[14] and Dewey himself had been thinking about the implications as early as 1929.[15] He refers to a discussion between physicists Albert Einstein and Niels Bohr, who took very different positions, remarking of Einstein that: "in contrast with his transactional (i.e. free and open) treatment of physical phenomena, Einstein remained strongly self-actional (i.e. traditionally constrained) in his attitude towards man's activity in scientific enterprise", contrasting this with Bohr's position: "a much freer view of the world that has man as an active component within it, rather than one with man by fixed dogma set over against it".[16]

Einstein and Bohr had been debating metaphysical issues raised by quantum mechanics, such as wave-particle duality, which had shown that the nature of the observed phenomena changes with the way the experiment is set up. Werner Heisenberg had proposed the "uncertainty principle" to resolve this wave-particle dualism, which focuses on what knowledge we are able to have about a particle's properties. Bohr's proposed solution was more ontological. His principle of complementarity suggests that properties such as momentum and position have no physical reality independent of the observer, and that descriptions such as "wave" and "particle" refer not to independent physical objects, but to different and mutually exclusive phenomena. For Bohr, as for Dewey, we are ourselves part of the reality we are investigating. There is no clear separation between ourselves as investigating subjects and the world as investigated object. They constitute a whole, and the interaction between the observer and the observed is also an inseparable part of the phenomenon. The idea of the experiment being independent of mind or independent of context is an illusion.

The American physicist and feminist scholar Karen Barad takes her inspiration from Bohr to develop her theory of agential realism,[17] however, while Bohr focuses on physics and laboratory experiments, Barad extends his insights of entangled subjects and objects more generally, regarding them not as a particular property of nature, but "the very nature of nature".[18] She has coined the term intra-action, a key concept of agential realism, to emphasise the mutual participation of subject and object. Some of her ideas link closely to Dewey's notion of transaction via their mutual interest in Bohr.[19]

14 Dewey had learned about the breaking developments in quantum mechanics in the late 1920s first hand from his daughter Jane, who had conducted post-doctoral research with Niels Bohr, Werner Heisenberg, Erwin Schrodinger and other physicists in Copenhagen.

15 When he wrote *Quest for Certainty*.

16 John Dewey and Arthur F. Bentley, *Knowing and the Known* (Boston, Beacon Press, 1960, first published 1949): 108.

17 Karen Michelle Barad, *Meeting the Universe Halfway: Quantum Physics and the Entanglement of Matter and Meaning* (Durham NC: Duke University Press, 2007)

18 Ibid., 6.

19 Matz Hammarström, "On the Concepts of Transaction and Intra-action", The Third Nordic Pragmatism Conference, Uppsala, 1-2 June 2010. https://internt. ht.lu.se/media/documents/persons/MatzHammarstrom/On_the_Concepts_of_ Transaction_and_Intra_action.pdf

As with Bohr, Barad considers herself as a scientific realist, albeit in a new form. In a similar way to that argued by Ghag and Biswas in their conversation, her view is that, by understanding that the scientist is always part of the apparatus, this can make scientific work more accurate and more rigorous. She believes that this kind of "social construction of science" critique actually makes for better and more credible science.

Forming the great community

Dewey relates the role of art, science and experience to the goal of achieving a genuine democratic society.[20] If society is to be transformed into a "great community", as he calls it, the social transmission of knowledge and tools is needed, which requires difficult kinds of inquiries combined with a "subtle, delicate, vivid and responsive art of communication".[21] Art works as a universal mode of language. Although a specific artwork may not speak to a particular person, art surrounds us and, in its myriad forms, it remains at the centre of human experience.

The art of science, or of history, or politics or any artform all have the same "material": they are made up of the interactions between the live creature and its environment.[22] None are context- and culture-free. Scientific research responds to specific problems, and thoughtful scientists understand the social significance of their work. Science is not just the accumulation of facts, or of endless measurements. For science to play its full role in society or community, it needs to remain connected to the conditions that inspired it. The danger of scientists failing to consider the moral, social and technological implications of their research means that science "becomes brutal and mechanical".[23]

Physics, and science in general, needs to realise the implications that science is done by humans for humans, and to realise the implications of this. More vitally, it must reconnect with the arts of life, rather than choosing to remain "on an altar in a temple ... to be approached only with peculiar rites",[24] where, for many people, it will continue to be regarded merely, and dangerously, as a remote and obscure body of odd belief systems and codes that have little to do with everyday life.

Bibliography

Barad, Karen Michelle, *Meeting the Universe Halfway: Quantum Physics and the Entanglement of Matter and Meaning* (Durham NC: Duke University Press, 2007)
CERN, "Interview with James Wells (Collide@CERN) for Swiss Info" (2012), https://videos.cern.ch/record/1483712.

20 John Dewey, *Experience and Nature* (London: George Allen & Unwin, 1929)
21 Ibid., 184.
22 John Dewey, *Experience and Nature* (Where: Who, 1929).
23 Ibid., 382.
24 Ibid., 381.

Dewey, John, *The Public and its Problems* (New York: H. Holt and Company, 1927).

Dewey, John, *Experience and Nature* (London: George Allen & Unwin, 1929)

Dewey, John, *Art as Experience* (New York: Minton, Balch & Company, 1934).

Dewey, John, and Arthur F. Bentley, *Knowing and the Known* (Boston, Beacon Press, 1960, first published 1949).

Hammarström, Matz. "On the Concepts of Transaction and Intra-action", The Third Nordic Pragmatism Conference, Uppsala, 1-2 June 2010. https://internt.ht.lu.se/media/documents/persons/MatzHammarstrom/On_the_Concepts_of_Transaction_and_Intra_action.pdf

Hasse, Cathrine. "Cultural Models of Physics: An Analysis of Historical Connections Between Hard Sciences, Humanities and Gender in Physics". In *University Science and Mathematics Education in Transition*, edited by Ole Skovsmose, Paola Valero and Ole Ravn Christensen, 109-132. Boston, MA.: Springer, 2009.

Pugh, Kevin J., and Mark Girod. "Science, Art, and Experience: Constructing a Science Pedagogy From Dewey's Aesthetics." *Journal of Science Teacher Education* 18, no. 1 (2007): 9-27. http://www.jstor.org/stable/43156404.

Traweek, Sharon, *Beamtimes and Lifetimes* (Boston MA.: Harvard University Press, 1988).

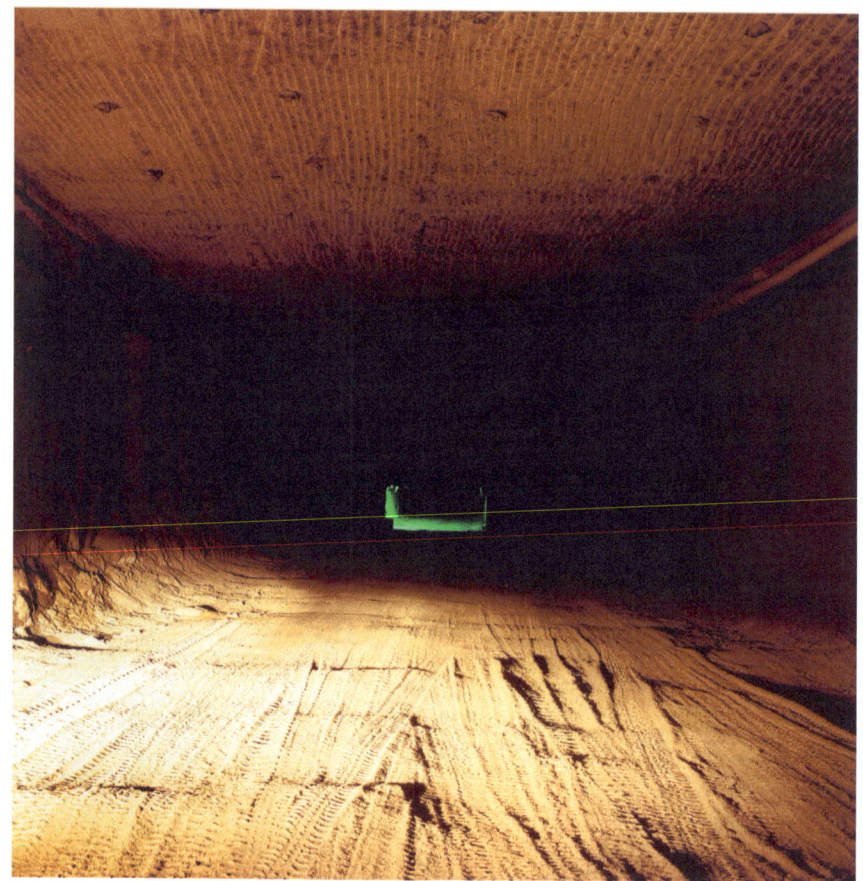

Fig. 1 — Fiona Crisp, *Safe Haven*, 2010
Giclée print from colour transparency
Image courtesy the artist and Matt's Gallery, London

Material Sight — *Fiona Crisp*

Material Sight is a body of cross-disciplinary research that
has been evolved at three world-leading research facilities for
experimental and theoretical physics. The project uses non-
documentary photography, film and sound to explore how lay
publics might encounter the extreme perceptual remoteness
of fundamental science by connecting us to the material
environments where physics is performed.

Sited within a mountain in central Italy, the Laboratori Nazionali
del Gran Sasso is the world's largest underground research
centre for particle physics; by contrast Boulby Underground
Laboratory occupies the UK's deepest working mine. Both
environments are distinguished by their powerful materiality yet
the science being performed in them is abstract, imperceptible and
often lies beyond a lay public's cognitive and imaginative grasp. The
scales, distances and time-frames that fundamental physics and
cosmology trade in, from the sub-atomic to the multiverse, cause
a kind of vertigo when we try and scale them against the measure
of our bodies or the range of our perceptual senses. So how could
we have a haptic relation to fundamental physics? How can we, in
Roger Malina's term, make science intimate?

I first gained access to Boulby Underground Laboratory in
2009 whilst making work for the exhibition *Subterannia*.[1] At a
depth of over a kilometre, the mine extracts potash, polyhalite
and rock salt from tunnels reaching out under the North Sea to
distances of up to fifteen kilometres. Visiting the Laboratory is a
deeply physical experience, starting with the air pressure and
noise during the long descent in the lift cage alongside the mine
workers and continuing with the intense heat and dust as you
follow the tunnel system out to the laboratory. The depth of rock
shields against cosmic rays, crucial to create the "quiet" conditions
that the experiments at Boulby rely on, but it is the environment's
intense materiality that forcibly strikes the visitor, not least
because this sensory-driven experience is in diametric opposition
to the imperceptible life of the experiments themselves. Inside the
temperature-controlled, dust-free environment of the laboratory
itself, technology mediates signals and data at scales that move us
out beyond the body's perceptual and cognitive reach.

This paradoxical relationship, between the material presence
of the environment on the one hand and the extreme perceptual
remoteness of the science on the other, became the conceptual
core around which the project *Material Sight* developed. I found
myself questioning whether the material environment where
fundamental physics is performed could, in some way, be a conduit
to cognitive understanding, or at least create an intimacy that
could lead lay-publics to "connect" to the areas of fundamental
science that are traditionally so hard for non-scientists to
imaginatively or cognitively grasp.

1   Fiona Crisp, *Subterrania*, BALTIC Centre for Contemporary Art, Impressions
    Gallery, Newlyn Art Gallery (2009–2010).

Importantly, these questions were posed through the prism of photography, particularly my ongoing exploration regarding the limits and capabilities of photography and its ability (or not) to embody phenomenological presence. As the writer James Elkins has observed in relation to astronomy, "Intuition gives out when magnitude passes a certain point."[2] *Material Sight* seeks to counter this tendency toward perceptual vertigo by re-introducing us to a bodily relation to physical spaces, thus bringing the science back within our world as experience; what the philosopher Edmund Husserl in 1936 called, the "Life-World". In this respect, I am asking if photography and the moving image can *embody* the spaces of experimental science and present them back to scientists and nonscientists alike, not as illustrations of the technical sublime but as sites of phenomenological encounter.

Like Boulby, Laboratori Nazionali del Gran Sasso (LNGS) is characterized by its powerful materiality yet the two sites differ in their relative architectural scales. The three vast underground Halls at LNGS were mined in the 1980s when the autostrade tunnel passing underneath the Gran Sasso mountain range was excavated. Interestingly, the facility sits in alignment to CERN, the world's most well known facility for high-energy physics, in an uncanny anticipation of the famous CERN Neutrinos to Gran Sasso (CNGS) beam sent from the Large Hadron Collider at CERN to Gran Sasso to test Neutrino oscillation.[3] The huge OPERA experiment at LNGS (2003-2012) was built to detect the beam using a "target" of 156,000 "bricks", each made from large-format photographic film (nuclear emulsion) interleaved with lead sheets and weighing approximately 9kg. Now disassembled, OPERA retains an archive of a fraction of the bricks for future research (see Fig.2). Three of these bricks sit in my studio in the North East of England exerting an intense physical and conceptual presence. I do not possess the advanced scanning technology to 'read' the emulsion plates but the sealed contents of each brick holds the *potential* (albeit highly unlikely) trace of a neutrino "event". To hold the dense weight of the brick and consider that ineffable neutrino beam is a powerful experience.

During my repeated visits to Gran Sasso, I became increasingly interested in how the experiments "performed" their conceptual and philosophical potentialities and, more specifically, how the methodologies from wider culturally (rather than scientifically) oriented spheres could interact with and reveal these potentialities. The Large Volume Detector (LVD) at LNGS is a case in point. Essentially an underground observatory built to study neutrinos from core-collapse supernovae, the LVD has been monitoring our galaxy since 1992. Built on a modular system of blocks with its hundreds of photo-multiplier tubes surface mounted, the LVD is

2   James Elkins, *Six stories from the end of representation*. (Palo Alto, CA: Stanford University Press, 2008)

3   The Oscillation Project with Emulsion-tRacking Apparatus (OPERA) was an instrument used in a scientific experiment for detecting tau neutrinos from muon neutrino oscillations. The experiment was a collaboration between CERN and LNGS and uses the CERN Neutrinos to Gran Sasso (CNGS) neutrino beam.

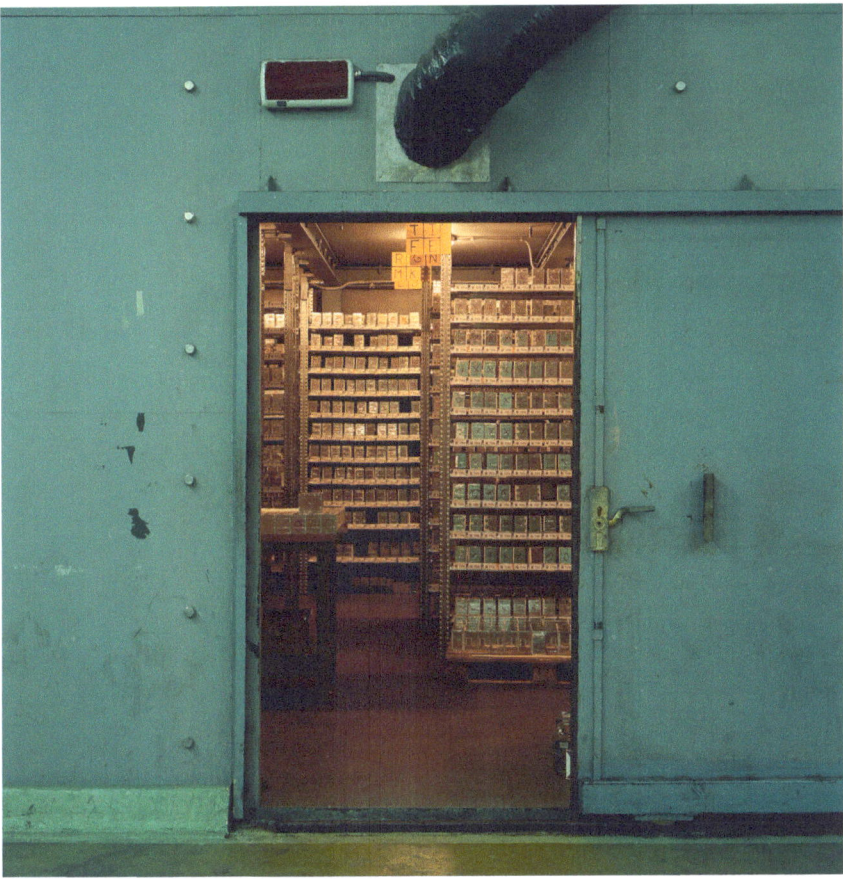

like a multi-storey cityscape that one can walk through and around, differentiating it from most subsequent detectors that have sealed and inaccessible cores encased in various forms of lead, copper and purified water shields. The LVD's permeability allowed me to perform an active exploration of the experiment's interior, moving through, around and along the corridors and levels with a film camera.

The third site for *Material Sight* was the combined facilities at Durham University that include The Centre for Advanced Instrumentation (CfAI) and The Institute of Computational Cosmology (ICC). The workshops of the CfAI, including the Precision Optics Laboratory, was where I was able to produce some of the most detailed, closely shot footage for the project, paying durational witness to the engineering processes involved in producing instruments for remote sensing and vision (see Fig. 4). Many of these instruments, such as spectrometers and telescopes, provide the data used by The Institute of Computational Cosmology for researching the origins and evolution of the universe and for constructing visualisations, such as The Millennium Simulation,

Fig. 2 — Fiona Crisp, *LNGS: OPERA Archive*, 2018
Giclée print from colour transparency
Image courtesy the artist and Matt's Gallery, London

using their super-computer, COSMA. Given my questions about the limits and capabilities of photography and its indexical relationship to the world, I was really interested to engage scientists at the ICC in conversations about working between observed, enhanced and constructed imagery. I also wanted to ask how such models and simulations are culturally received; for example, some visualisations retain an indexical link to the observed cosmos

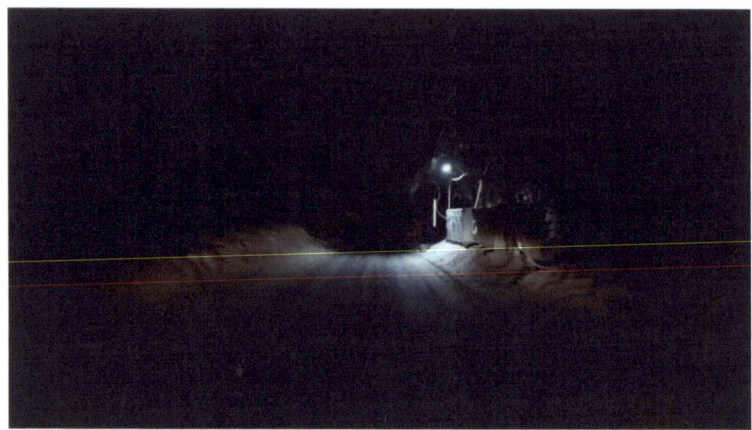

Fig. 3 — Fiona Crisp, *Boulby Mine*, 2018
Single Channel Video
Image courtesy the artist and Matt's Gallery, London

whilst other simulations are built entirely from numerical data and therefore have interesting parallels with virtual reality. As Professor Richard Bower remarked during a recorded discussion with myself and his colleague Dr Mark Swinbank at the ICC, "I'm trying to make a universe, and then be part of that universe, even though it doesn't exist".[4]

An important sub-text to *Material Sight* as a project is the challenge it makes to the model of art as illustrator in art/science collaborations. Far too frequently "science is understood as complete, and as needing only to be communicated or applied, while art provides the means through which the public can be assembled and mobilized on behalf of science".[5] In contrast, my interest is in framing visual practice not as an illustrator or interpreter of science, but as an active contributor to emergent technologies that are constituted from a hybrid mix of the technological, the sociopolitical, and the cultural.[6] Essentially, I am advocating the *production of knowledge through looking*; in this respect, my work is premised on visual arts practice as a producer rather than an

4   Richard Bower, Fiona Crisp, Mark Swinbank, *Visualisations in Cosmology* [online] (2016). Available at: https://materialsight.wordpress.com/.
5   Georgina Born and Andrew Barry, "ART-SCIENCE", *Journal of Cultural Economy* 3, no. 1 (2010): 103.
6   See activities of *The Cultural Negotiation of Science Research Group* at https://www.cnos.org.uk/about.

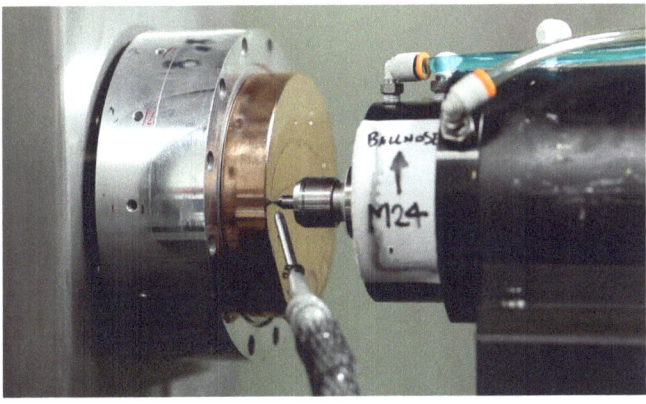

Fig. 4 — Fiona Crisp, *Precision Optics Laboratory: Ballnose*, 2013
Single channel video
Image courtesy the artist and Matt's Gallery, London

illustrator of knowledge, placing artistic production in the spaces where experimental and theoretical science is performed and foregrounding the "site" or laboratory as a social, cultural, and political space where meaning is shaped and constructed rather than received or observed.[7]

This approach necessitates *trust*. I have needed to build working relationships with scientists so that they are comfortable with me observing their environments and working practices. Further to this, and perhaps more challenging, I have engaged them in recorded dialogue that brings language and methodologies from my own sphere, creating a series of recorded interviews that are amassing to form a contextual archive for the project.[8] I take still and moving imagery – the building of "knowledge through looking" already mentioned - often returning repeatedly to a site before I understand what the work needs to be. It is important to note that my work is not concerned with imparting subject-specific knowledge; just as I avoid any claim to a documentary subject, I also eschew the notion that my visual practice in any way demonstrates ideas within science and technology. My interest is in whether photography and film can contribute to a cultural negotiation of "extreme" science and technology, not through being utilised as a documentary tool, but by being used as a language that mirrors science's probing of the furthest reaches of imagination and comprehension. Central to this thinking is the suspension of our desire for empirical knowledge to allow for what I have referred to in earlier writing as "productive doubt".[9] This could be useful in the context of scientists understanding how advances in their field are culturally connected as well as for lay

7   Robert Doubleday, "Organizing accountability: Co-production of technoscientific and social worlds in a nanoscience laboratory", *Area* 39, no. 2 (2007): 166–75.
8   See *Material Sight* project website at https://materialsight.wordpress.com/.
9   Fiona Crisp, "Negative Capability: Imaging and Imagining Fundamental Science Through Productive Doubt" *GeoHumanities* 1, no. 1 (2015): 2.

publics being able to imaginatively engage with those advances. Furthermore, productive doubt could provide artists and other cultural producers with a tool to think through the implications of scientific and technological advances *via practice* and might encourage the evolution of collaborative working relationships that genuinely advance knowledge across the arts, fundamental science, and social science simultaneously.

But, ultimately, the research resides within the audience's experiential encounter with the work itself. Through large-scale photographs, moving image and visceral soundscape, *Material Sight* enacts the "endeavour" of fundamental science - experimental physics, felt in the gut.

Material Sight was generously supported by a Leverhulme Research Fellowship 2016-2018. The exhibition opened at the Northern Gallery for Contemporary Art, Sunderland March 2018 and toured to Arts Catalyst, London June 2018. The exhibition and events were funded by Arts Council England and the Science & Technology Facilities Council.

Bibliography

Bower, Richard, Fiona Crisp, and Mark Swinbank. *Visualisations in Cosmology* [online]. (2016) Available at: https://materialsight.wordpress.com/

Born, Georgina, and Andrew Barry, "ART-SCIENCE", *Journal of Cultural Economy* 3, no. 1 (2010): 103-119.

Crisp, Fiona, "Negative Capability: Imaging and Imagining Fundamental Science Through Productive Doubt", *GeoHumanities* 1, no. 1 (2015).

Doubleday, Robert, "Organizing accountability: Co-production of technoscientific and social worlds in a nanoscience laboratory", *Area* 39, no. 2 (2007): 166–75.

Elkins, James, *Six stories from the end of representation*. (Palo Alto, CA: Stanford University Press, 2008).

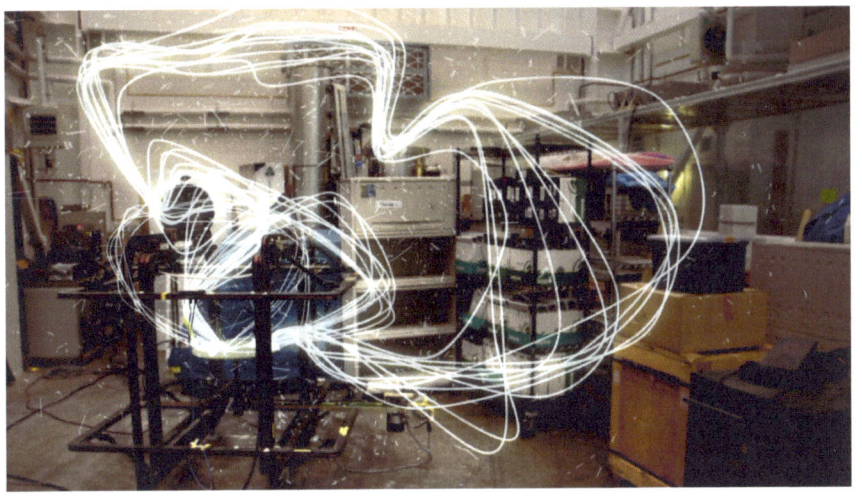

Semiconductor, *Magnetic Movie*, 2007
HD single channel

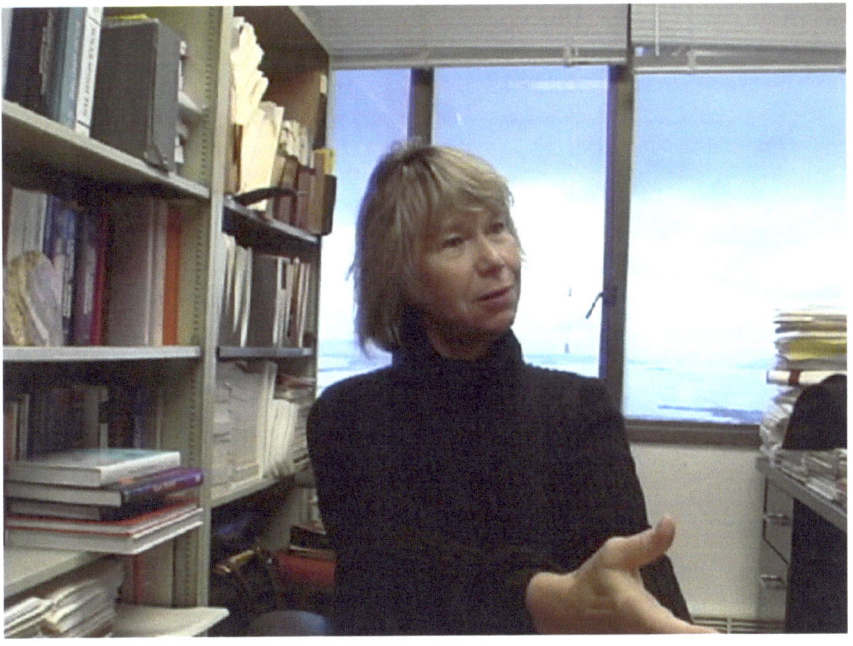

Semiconductor, *Do You Think Science...*, 2006
SD single channel

Why Do We Do Science?
— *Suchitra Sebastian*

A transcript of a talk given in October 2017 at the Institute of Physics

The kind of physics I work on involves emergent quantum phenomena. This is the physics of certain materials in which exotic quantum phenomena manifest at the very large scale. One of the things I work on is superconductivity and what is special about these materials is that, when you cool them to an almost magical superconducting temperature, electrons pair up and coalesce into a giant quantum wave whereby they're all perfectly coordinated. In these materials, electricity can flow perfectly with absolutely no loss of energy, current flowing through a superconducting ring for example would continue to flow for the age of the universe. An example of a very large superconducting ring is the ring of magnets at the particle accelerator at CERN.

I look at emergent properties – what phenomena emerge at this macroscopic quantum level that don't exist when there are only single electrons. To some extent we understand this, but we still struggle to understand how the emergent can be fundamental. We're used to breaking particles down to the smallest we can get, and then that's the fundamental. We're less familiar with a language where electrons come together to form emergent phenomena and that's the fundamental. What I find really exciting about this field is that it's very experimental. Most often, rather than there being a theory to describe how these phenomena work, it's often empirically driven. One of the ways I use to discover new quantum phases of matter is to take a material, cool it down to low temperatures, put a giant magnetic field on it or press it under high pressures, and find that it transforms into something else. I call this quantum alchemy. It's almost like you've gone into a different universe. Every day in the laboratory, you have no idea what you're going to find, you have no idea what your material is going to do.

This is the kind of physics I do, and the kind of physics I've chosen to do is very much a function of who I am, and the fact that I enjoy discovering. I actually enjoy the mystery, and the not-knowing even more than knowing. This is how I view life. This is how I view travel. Physics is just one aspect of what I do, which just embodies my approach to exploration and discovery.

This is something that is often missed in physics, the idea that who you are is at the core of how you do physics. There is this conceit that physics is so objective and so abstract that you could take the physicist out of it and you'd still have this pure, rarefied, morally neutral discipline. I think this is a misleading notion. The progress of science will always be shaped by the scientist – who they are, and why they do what they do. Anyone claiming that you can take the physicist out of the picture and leave an unchanged, objective, abstract physics is simply mentally imposing a physicist of a certain type and envisaging a certain way of doing physics.

To do physics in a different way, and to bring in aspects of you as a person into physics, challenges conventional thinking. It requires a lot of strength of character to insist that you will do physics in the way you conceive it, in a way that is different from how it is usually conceived in the physics world. This is why it's so important to bring art and science together: in order to be able to view the world through different lenses.

To give some background to how I reached physics, my undergraduate degree was in physics, but it was in a liberal art college. I did physics, but I also studied literature and languages, and I just assumed this was how one looked at the world, through thinking about it in different ways. I really enjoyed physics. I enjoyed this aspect of discovery, just finding things out, which is incredibly exciting. But I was not convinced about the idea of physicists, because they seemed incredibly insular and they had this idea that the whole world was viewed through one lens. For a while I tried running away from physics, doing other things – business school, management consultancy – and then I came back to physics, but with an idea that maybe I could try and do it differently.

I went to grad school at Stanford, and I had the luxury to choose whatever I wanted to do, so I did a lot of theatre as well as physics, and I was also very involved in anti-war activism. But if you're trying to become a physicist, at some point they demand that physics is your whole life, and it's quite difficult to struggle against this. They also demand that you are the kind of physicist that they expect you to be, which is their kind of physicist - who has gravitas, who apparently does nothing but physics. Subconsciously, without recognising it, I ended up thinking - well, I'll accommodate what they demand of me and that bit of me that does physics, that's the only part of me that I'll use in the physics world. I tried to compartmentalise, and separate the different aspects of me.

Interestingly, the recognition that I wasn't bringing my whole self to physics, became clearest when I started engaging more with general audiences. When you talk to the public, it's really clear when they're not interested in what you're saying - and they're not interested if you talk about your physics in an abstract way, carefully removing yourself from it (as you're supposed to do in the physics world). People can tell when you're not bringing your whole self to it, and they're totally not interested in that really exciting thing that you do if they don't get why you, as a person, are passionate about it. Within physics, there's a conceit that you can separate the person out, but as soon as you go out into the world, people see instantly that there is no such thing. And if you don't bring your whole self to it, they recognise this lack of authenticity. This is when I started to bring those two parts of me, that I had separated out in order to do physics, back together. Those different aspects of me: the part of me that thinks more broadly and is interested in other ways of exploring the world, and the part that views the world through a science lens. The fascinating thing was that when I brought my whole self to physics, it made me a much better physicist, it reignited my passion for discovery and exploring in new ways, which is core to the physics I do.

I think it is vital for science to rediscover an integrated approach – between the scientist and the science, and between different ways of viewing the world. First, it's important to think back to why it is we do physics. We do science essentially because we're human and because we inquire. We want to know about the world around us. We want to know about our place in the world and the connection between us and the universe. This is why we start inquiring. This is why we come to science. Science and the essence of being human - why we inquire, these are inseparable.

I think increasingly science has allowed itself to be defined and valued by what it is useful for. Every time you write a grant proposal, every time you justify your existence as a physicist, it's just about what it is your science is useful for, what technology it can be used for. Of course there is a pragmatic reason for this, and science and technology are indeed instrumental for making the world a better place. But it is limiting for science to allow itself to be boxed-in in that way and not to emphasise its crucial value as an essential element of the human condition, part of being and a part of inquiring. The sole emphasis on a utilitarian reason for doing science risks losing the really important blue skies exploration which is where earthshattering discoveries are actually made, which change the way we view the world. And we're losing out on a lot of people who think more holistically or creatively. It's really important, therefore, to bring art back into science, develop a dialogue between art and science on an equal footing, as two ways of inquiring that work synergistically together, and to encourage a holistic notion of why we inquire.

The separation between the essence of being human, and the pursuit of science leads to another troubling notion. One that invokes the superiority of science as the arbiter of truth; because it brings knowledge and facts together and that it is the only discipline able to do this. The inference then is that morally unsuitable decisions are being made because they're not based on scientific facts. That's not the problem. The problem is that we've allowed science to become a space of moral neutrality, in which facts are separated from the decisions about how we use those facts. We need to put the human back at the centre of science. Without acknowledging the sanctity of the human, how can we ask questions of what is good for our planet, or make decisions that won't destroy the ecosystem. Of course science is capable of bettering our lives, but it is equally capable of causing incredible devastation - one has only to look at history. To make decisions on how we use scientific knowledge, we need to bring science fully into the entire social construct and acknowledge the human at the centre of science. It is deathly to imagine we can divorce science from the overarching moral imperative that is core to our humanity.

Truth is not static, and truth is not just about facts that only an expert scientist can capture. If we go back and look at how truth has been conceived by various thinkers through history, it is very different to the static notion we conceive in this technological, science-driven age. In a different era of physics, Maxwell, who discovered electromagnetism, wrote poetry as well and one of his poems has this line: "Let old words new truth inspire ...". The idea is that truth is not static, it is ever evolving. The philosopher, Heidegger, also had this notion of truth as active. He writes of

"The unconcealment of being" - this is never a state that is merely present but rather a happening. Gandhi also came at truth the same way, noting: "Truth is not passive or inactive. It is an active movement." Reducing truth to something that's static, and that only science can probe, is both limiting and dangerous. Science likes to say that it's morally superior because it's morally neutral. I don't think there is any such thing. We need to get away from this notion if science is to be used in human progress, to advance inquiry.

So how do we put the human back into the pursuit of science? I'd like to move away from this idea of science as merely useful as an advancer of technology, and away from a reductionist way of thinking. All it does is limit our exploration of the world, and objectify and reduce the world to something that can be calculated. What makes us human is also dissolved in that objectification.

To get away from this, we need several things. We need different ways of looking at the world. We need to bring art back into the realm of science. We need diversity in science that allows for people who do things in different ways, so that science is not just the realm of the mythical scientist we construct in our mind's eye, but it is exploration in different areas.

Having a diversity of people in physics is essential to be able to do physics in different ways. To achieve this, our way of learning needs to be changed. The reason that only one type of person ends up being a physicist is that, when we learn physics, it's reduced to doing a problem set and finding an answer. If the answer matches the problem, we get a good grade and that allows us to go and do physics. What happens to all the people who are not excited by that way of doing science? What happens to all the people who enjoy exploring? Of course, physicists need to understand the framework for doing physics and the framework of the mathematics that underlie it, but more than that they need to be motivated to ask why, and to ask why not? Why does something work in the way it does and not another way? It's not just a mathematical formula.

Bringing diverse people into physics, and encouraging ways of learning that bring all our humanity into science, are really important.

A further note on diversity in physics

This was said by Suchitra Sebastian in answer to a question on women in physics, at an event at Arts Catalyst, October 2017.

I think anyone who's not the majority, not just demographically but also in terms of personality type that does science, finds the culture of physics difficult. I'm not sure why the field has evolved the way that it has - my guess is historical, sociological reasons - but the way it is at the moment, it's very self-selecting. People in the field assume that to be a good physicist you have to be "like them". In their own mind, they're not selecting for anything other than good physics, but in reality of course they're selecting for a plethora of characteristics that are to do with the person and not just the physics that they do.

If you're in that segment of people who have been self-selected, you don't question this. You just think that it's the norm. For example, I was at a conference of philosophy and physics and I noticed that it was again all male and I was talking to some guy and he said "Oh, did you notice the demographic?!", and I said "Yeah!", and he goes "It was all old people!". And I said "Well, actually, I noticed it was all guys", and he goes "I didn't notice that ... but that means I'm gender neutral, right?". And I said "No ...". I asked "If it was all women, would you have noticed?" and he said "Oh, yeah, I would have noticed".

That's the point. They think they're gender neutral, but in reality, they're conditioned for everyone to be like themselves. And if you're not like that, then immediately there's a conflict in trying to reconcile your identity with the identity that's expected of you in that field.

The Joy of Simplicity — *Tara Shears*

There is something about simplicity that draws me to physics. In a very general sense, I find simplicity appealing and reassuring. Perhaps it's that the world is complicated, that when you absorb everything around you the variety of objects and behaviour and sounds and textures can be overwhelming. Identifying connections, seeing underlying links like an invisible chain, and understanding why things happens gives me a way to order the world in a way that can fit inside my thoughts. It's not that I don't celebrate complexity and the richness of my surroundings. It's that simultaneously seeing the hidden dimension of causation, the mechanics behind the universe, this is what gives me awe and wonder and where I see beauty.

Particle physics is full of people like me. Our science deconstructs the universe to a sparse number of tiny fundamental elements whose behaviour is encapsulated in universal laws of nature. We see patterns and symmetries in behaviour and use them to derive ever-simpler descriptions of what goes on. At the moment we've identified twelve fundamental particles and four fundamental forces. It's too many. We think there should be fewer. It's a level of detail in the universe that we can never see or touch directly and a bias to think this should be so. But to see an underlying cause that explains why we see twelve particles, to glimpse a simpler heart, this is what drives us. For me, that glimpse is what I would spend my life working toward. It's the moment when your vision clears, where your tension disappears, that moment that you feel the connections forming the universe to be part of you too.

I find this joy in simplicity affects everything. Throughout school, I studied literature as well as science and mathematics. It's always nagged me that these subjects are perceived to be so different when they have so many similarities at their heart. Mathematics is a language with pure economy of expression. It has a beauty and elegance that rests in the perfect way it can encapsulate a relation – a literally perfect way, with no alternative expression possible that doesn't alter the meaning. I love the richness of language in literature, but more than anything I love the tautness and ability to capture a feeling or view or moment in a handful of words. When words are just right, when they are a perfect choice, they give me that same feeling of insight and awe and warmth and clarity. For me, poetry is not dissimilar to mathematics in the big picture of what it does. Neither is music. And neither is art. In all of them I'm drawn to the economy by which they can say so much, and the vastness of what that means.

Simplicity drew me to particle physics. Simplicity informs my daily work, gives me that compulsion that makes work become an all-abiding interest and lets me sense the underlying working of the universe. It lets me touch on what is eternal and fundamental and beyond my ability to experience, through science and art and music too. It's a very human feeling, to need this connection, and peculiar to think that a very human need has shaped my area of science. It makes you wonder sometimes just how independent of us our understanding of the universe is. Despite our efforts to be objective, perhaps it's ultimately a reflection of what we need to be there.

Bias, for a scientist, is a crime. I wonder sometimes how equipped we really are to differentiate what we want from what we see. I wonder how artists evaluate when they have reached their truth of expression too.

I've realised that our way of working is unusual. We work in huge collectives of thousands of scientists who are distributed around the globe and stay in touch by regular videoconferencing.

We work on our experiments as (unpaid) volunteers in whatever time we have away from teaching and other duties. We make all our data available to every member of the experiment. We continuously evaluate and critique each other's findings for bias. Nothing goes out without everyone's approval. We are all authors of every experimental publication regardless of who did the work, listed in alphabetical order. That encourages us to cross-check again, because all of our reputations are on the line if results are wrong. From the outside, we are all our experiment and nothing more individual than that.

On the inside of course, things are different. Everyone would like to make a discovery; everyone wants to be first to have that moment of insight. There are external pressures - success wins future funding. There is ambition and there is tension. After all, we are people too. It is so easy to write in terms of "we" to describe our behaviour, because ultimately we all act according to the same rules. We all want to understand more. We all know we need each other's expertise to get there. We give respect according to how good someone's work is, rather than who they are (not being paid releases you from hierarchy). Our individual ambition becomes ambition for what we can all achieve together. Bad behaviour doesn't normally last for long; noone wants to be thrown off an experiment. You need to challenge orthodoxy from within if you find something that needs to be improved.

To us, this way of working sometimes seems slow and clunky, but we haven't found anything better. What motivates us all is what led me to my science and what I search for in everything. It's that moment of quiet stillness that overshadows chaos, when you realise you see further than ever. It's the awe of being momentarily part of something vast where you are insignificant, and yet you see it. It's the joy of simplicity.

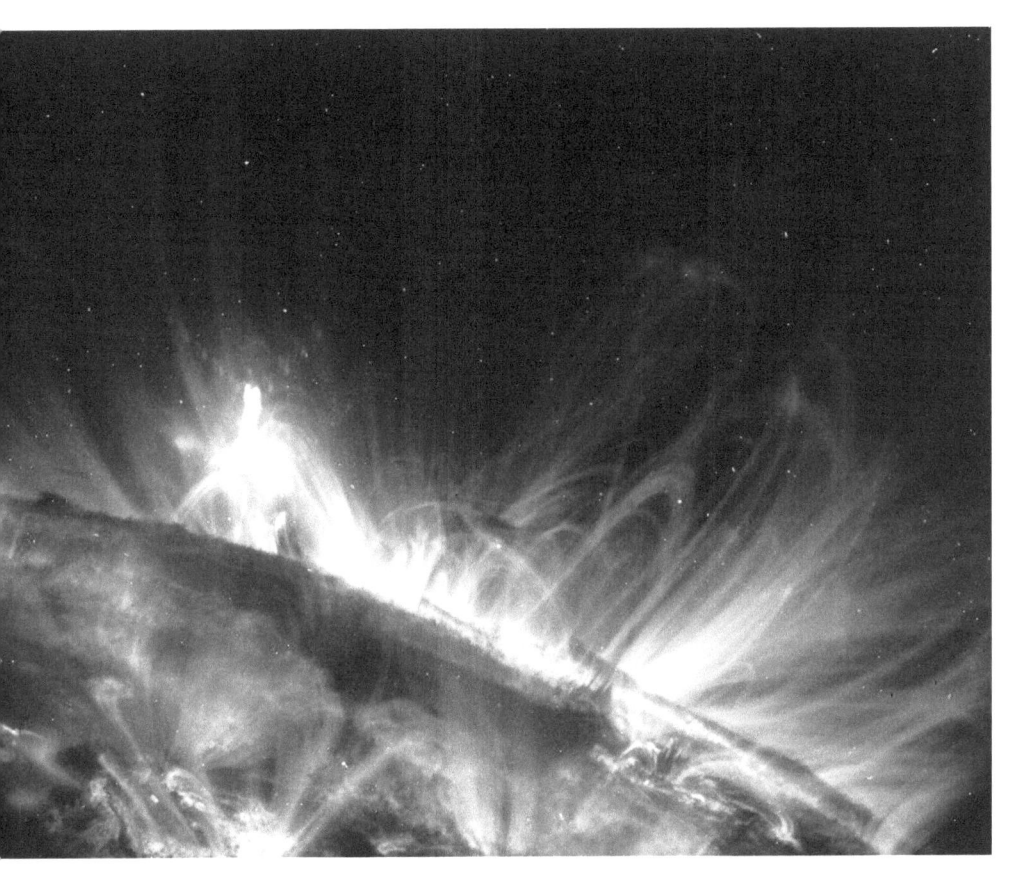

Semiconductor, *Brilliant Noise*, 2006
SD / HD / single channel + multi-channel versions

Contemplative Science
— *Chamkaur Ghag and Ansuman Biswas*

A conversation between Dr Chamkaur Ghag, astroparticle physicist and dark matter researcher, and Ansuman Biswas, artist and musician, took place at Arts Catalyst in January 2018. These are edited transcripts of that conversation.

Chamkaur Ghag — David Bohm[1] talks about how 'culture' shares the same root as 'cultivate' but also 'cult'.

Ansuman Biswas — In Sanskrit, the word for culture is 'bhavana' which has the same root as the English 'to be' and 'to become'. Contemplative practice, meditation practice, is the cultivation of something. You're trying to encourage the growth of a particular way of looking. There's this idea that things are becoming all the time but that we can consciously direct the course of how they go, so there's an awareness that there's a culture. On the other hand, in science there seems to be this idea that it's free of culture: "We're finding universal laws."

CG — As an aspiration, I think that trying to go after universal laws is ok. But it's the direction of science ... not being conscious of what it is that's being cultivated, what's being created, and thinking that it's all fine because it's mathematically sound. Science becomes a thoughtless practice through how much thought is involved, nonstop thinking, which means there's a continual perpetuation of something without any reflection. The speed at which things are progressing is an indication that there's very little reflection. We're not asking ourselves, where are we heading, what are we doing? The only way we might do that, that I can think of, is to stop thinking. Meditative process has been profound for me: to stop, look, reflect and choose. And doing that doesn't feel like it's apart from the scientific method. I'm somebody who didn't do anything like meditation four or five years ago, back then, I would have completely disregarded anything that wasn't physical and tangible. But now I want to say, no, we need to stop and ask who do we want to be, what do we want - and is there a mechanism to choose? Because if we just carry on as we are, the planet can't cope with much more. Science has a role to play, both in terms of being complicit but also offering solutions.

For me, with meditation, the first realisation was really basic: "You mean my body isn't just this vehicle to carry my brain around?!"; that strain in my leg may be coupled to this stress I'm having at work. That realisation was spooky for me at the time. Now it's just obvious. Turns out my brain's connected to my leg!

Ansuman (laughing) — Who would have thought?

---

1   American scientist, who contributed unorthodox ideas to quantum theory, neuropsychology and the philosophy of mind.

CG — But the culture of certain areas of science is such that you can be divorced from all of that. You only need to think. It's the thought that matters. And your embodied relationships to what you're working on, or other people, anything like that, is sometimes not even secondary, it can be irrelevant.

AB — Or a hindrance.

CG — Or a hindrance. Absolutely.

AB — There's a dogma almost, which has been called scientific materialism. The idea that the physical is what matters. That's the object of study of science and it's completely independent of one's feelings or any mental component. But if we think about cultivating something ... the idea of becoming is that you go step by step. A plant, for example, grows cell by cell. Cultures grow through language. The language, in some sense, is the culture. In poetry the music of the language may be as important as whatever the poem's 'about'. I wonder how much you would think that mathematics is a language in that way?

CG — I'm not sure. Maths seems to be representing something so directly. There are structures that unfold using a set of rules, a geometry, that mathematics describes really very elegantly. Now whether it's still a metaphorical representation of something deeper, I've no idea.

AB — Do you think there's something essential about mathematics?

CG — It looks that way.

AB — The language of physics? But how does that relate to the physical world? When you get data about something, aren't you having to filter the data a lot in order to get something that's mathematically useable?

CG — Yes. We have to filter it, so that we can get something we can use and manipulate and understand. But there's still an awareness that there's a mathematical structure to all of it, even though we've got no hope of understanding it.

AB — You have faith that there's a mathematical structure.

CG — I think so, yes. Down to a level, down to the quantum realm, where we just can't say anything anymore because now it appears to be random. But even that randomness may have something underlying it. Personally, I have faith that there's some kind of ontological description that we might be able to use one day for what is going on at the quantum realm. I don't think everybody has that. A lot of scientists just get down to that level and say I've no idea what's going on, so I'm not going to question it or worry about it.

AB — Yet people must think about how they make decisions in the real world?

CG — I'm not sure we make decisions. I think there's this flow, and things are happening, and then there's this very interesting part of our brain - a lot of it seems to be the left hemisphere - that makes sense of it and provides this description of what happened and why. You can make a very simple elegant sweep of logic that justifies what you've just done. But you can see that your brain was firing half a second before you did it.

AB — A lot of the scientific method is about challenging that sort of intuitive understanding.

CG — Yes, but it's got lost. It has been useful - and it's still useful if you want to perpetuate the way we've been living, but that doesn't seem sensible anymore. It's costing too much. It may be that a new mode is starting to emerge, and that new mode isn't new at all. It's going back to what the scientific method is. It's not about trying to remove emotion or remove intuition, but trying to remove bias. However, bias has been confused with subjectivity and emotion. That's not it, I can still be a human and work on myself to see where my bias has come from.

We calibrate detectors and then you just wait for it to see something. Day to day, it's all about the detector and calibrating and removing bias. But then I started to realise, here I am, inherently constructed of biases, with my pre-conditioning and pre-programming, and I'm trying to tune this detector to be totally unbiased. How's that going to happen? We go about removing the biases from instruments, but we've still got to interpret the data. Until we've got to the point where we have machines that just take in the data and spit out the answer, it's still us. And we will have made those machines as well!

It's as Schrödinger[2] says in his book What is Life?; the Greeks understood that there would be a period of time when we started to know to use the tools, how to measure – and we're doing that to an incredible extent, we're measuring down to subatomic levels now - but in order to do that we've had to strip it from context. Now we've got to put it back into context. That's the next evolution of the scientific process. At the moment, it's just measure, measure, measure, measure. And when we're asked "what's the meaning?", there's no meaning because of the way we are applying the scientific method at present by isolating systems and stripping context.

AB — And you can get totally lost in that.

CG — I think we are, and it's manifesting in very different ways. Mental health in academia is one way. The constant thought, the constant stress of work, because you're never out of your

2 Erwin Schrödinger was a Nobel Prize-winning Austrian physicist who developed a number of fundamental results in the field of quantum theory.

head. Stepping back and looking doesn't mean that we've gone backwards. It just means we can see a bit more context. Are we done with all the measurement? Maybe not. But now we need to bring the beauty back. A lot of scientists – the best scientists actually – can still see the beauty in it, and there are a lot more of them than I thought. It's still what drives their curiosity. It's just that below them is the mainstream, the type of scientist that just sees it as a way of getting on with life.

AB — It's about the education system? That's where the culture is perpetuated.

CG — Yes, and an idea of what certain people are, that image. What's our idea of what Stephen Hawking is really saying? Or what was Einstein saying? Or Schrodinger or Feynman? When you really treat them as teachers, there's a whole lot more than just the equations that you need to pass the exam. That's part of the problem. The stress that's put on young people, so that they feel that they're achieving, that they can find their way in the world, is inhibiting their ability to change that world. There's a responsibility now for someone like myself to say to my students: feeling stressed? Go for a walk. Have you tried meditating?

AB — There's no doubt that yoga and meditation can be stress relievers, but it's a devaluation of their worth to treat them as stress relief. They're absolutely in line with the method that you were talking about. The elimination of bias. What happens with a proper contemplative science is that it continues exactly that process of eliminating bias, but in a very thorough way and with the whole system, including one's own observation. When you're doing a contemplative science, you're recognising that "I'm here and I want to know". Either we're looking for meaning (not simply data but meaningful data), or beauty, or the alleviation of pain and suffering. But we're looking for something. Acknowledging that, the project of the elimination of bias should continue, but with our whole being. It should be there within the culture of science.

CG — Some people spend their lives and careers studying the brain, the biomechanics of the body. I started with the outside - the stars and the planets. I think of some of my colleagues, and if you could look at the brain with their keenness of rationality. Their ability to just shed a bias is just phenomenal, because they follow the logic. If they caught a glimpse of this other tool, a detector, and realised they could play with this tool, that they could re-tune and calibrate it ... it's quite exciting really. But one of my fears is that to try to explain that too quickly, it can start to sound religious, which can come with a lot of negative connotations. I'm thinking of my own upbringing as a Sikh, when I started to realise that what we're doing is so far removed from this chap called Nanak, who just walked around learning things. And a few generations later, we're building golden temples! Or the church that doesn't allow somebody to truly understand what is meant by "turn the other cheek" or non-violence.

AB — Science has progressed extremely rapidly to the multi-billion pound industry and political project that it is now. It's not that long ago that someone was just using a drop of water to magnify a bit of leaf or a fly's wing, and now we've built these machines that have got more and more expensive and exploitative. Is it time to raze the whole thing to the ground?

CG — I thought so for a while, not about science, but about other areas. Now I look around and think: what do we need to change to solve world hunger? What do we need for homelessness? I don't need to burn down anything, it's just got to evolve, but that evolution isn't in the buildings, it's not in the structures, it's not even the technologies. It's in our intentions.

AB — So when we teach mathematics, why do we not teach the intention?

CG — Because we become very quickly disembodied, and there's no emotional connection. And that means that we're not susceptible to what our emotions and what our bodies are telling us about our environment. It becomes very easy to walk past a hungry homeless person and see them with our eyes, but not feel anything. The structures that allow that to happen are to some extent quite conscious. Science has a role to play here. Whilst we're off trying to figure out the universe, there are technological spinoffs that are used to sustain a dominant structure, a military structure. That technology keeps arriving not so much because there are scientists in the lab who say "I'm going to develop the most nasty bomb ever", but because they're just getting on with what they're doing. They're just not conscious of how complicit they are. In the sciences, we can be quite divorced from that, because our skill is being able to leave the body, get into the mind, and figure stuff out. And if we stay there and we don't ever drop back into our bodies and just be here, then we can continue to be exploited.

AB — But the resistance in the scientific culture is so strong to the "touchy feely", partly for good reason - this drive to eliminate bias, to impartiality and dispassionate apprehension of the truth. But you were saying you're seeing things in your department, people saying "well, I do practice yoga.". Are people starting to "come out"?

CG — Maybe. This conversation is a sort of an example of that. But the resistance is there. It's like we've built this building and we must keep the touchy feely out, so that people can just get on with measuring an atom. But having done that, we're realising there are no entrances, just brick walls. But that's not because people inside are averse to it anymore. The nice thing is that there are some very smart people on the inside and on the outside, and if they start to join up, we might realise that what we previously might have thought were weak spots – "ah, there's a little bit of art creeping in through this wall here – we need to shore it up!" – actually, that might be quite a strong point which allows something to start to come through. I don't think it's too late.

There's an interesting thing you were saying about the embodiment of the data. The neuroscience aspect is very interesting because of how we're handling big data now. This neural network that we're trying to mimic in a computer is nothing compared to the neural network that we already have. And it looks like you can plug in any sensory equipment. It doesn't have to be this eye, it could be an eye that can see in much broader wavelength spectra. What if the raw experimental data, say from a dark matter experiment, just went straight into your back through electrical stimulation, as is being done to help blindness with cameras feeding visual input into the skin? Would that help in alleviating the bias of what I choose to be relevant data and what I discard?

AB — One of the amazing things about homo sapiens is that we constantly expand our abilities to sense. This cognitive explosion that happened thousands of years ago, when language suddenly allowed us to be able to connect within groups of people. Now we have radio telescopes that can sense stuff that isn't part of our bodily apparatus, or instruments that can measure the tiniest perturbation so that we can sense gravity waves in a way that we can't with our body. Those are beautiful things. But they're beautiful only if they're integrated with our bodies. I think you're right to identify neuroscience as a frontier where a lot of work is happening. One aspect that quantum physics has clearly shown is that consciousness is somehow implicated in the material world. You can't avoid that anymore. And so we're looking in the brain. We're looking at neuroscience and neural networks and consciousness and data acquisition in new ways. There are people like Francisco Varela[3] and Antonio Damasio[4] talking about the bodily sensation of stuff that's happening the world. There's the Dalai Lama, an authoritative figure in Tibetan Buddhism, who's very interested in science and has been talking to Western-trained physicists. And within the Western tradition, Goethe and a sort of phenomenological approach to science, which does recognise that the body is central and the consciousness of the observer, is absolutely part of the system. There are routes that we can take to investigate these ideas.

CG — The Dalai Lama said that resistance can only hold when there is no data that compels a scientist to look. And now there's data. You can choose to ignore it, but then you're not doing science. The data is showing us, for example, that someone with a severed spinal column, watching a video of someone else training their leg muscle, brings about a tangible change in their own leg muscle. There's the data. It's hard to ignore. As the Dalai Lama says, it's through education that people can start to see. And when people can start to see the interconnection between the brain and the body, and the connection with how we live in a society ...

3   Chilean biologist, philosopher, and neuroscientist, best known for introducing
     the concept of autopoiesis to biology.
4   Portuguese-American neuroscientist.

AB — But education is a delicate process. When you're educating someone, you need to present things in just the right way, very gently. If a scientist wants to understand things through scientific materialism, then the language they're going to understand might be a graph of electrical spikes of particular neurones, so you show them that. And when they accept that, then you can say, well, you know there's this stuff happening – this chi moving through meridians of the body or ... But first show a graph.

CG — Absolutely. That's where rapid change is possible. We know very little about the brain, but now with this data coming in, the evidence is becoming undeniable. Here we are, living, but we don't really know how life originated. We know we're conscious, but we don't know where consciousness comes from. We're in this material universe, but we don't know what 96% of it is. It's clear that we don't know very much at all, so we shouldn't be closing things off. For a lot of scientists, they're fine with all that, it's just a process. So then, when you give them a physical graph, they tend not to reject it. There'll be a lot of scrutiny, sure, but once a scientist realises that they can't explain something fully with current theories, the opening up can be quite profound. Scientists, presented with evidence in a form they understand, can suddenly open themselves up. And while they may not want to go near words like "chi" or "tao", maybe they'll find they are describing the physical mechanisms these words were trying to point at. And once they open up ...

AB — Because a sceptic who's convinced is extremely powerful. In fact, scepticism is a keystone in contemplative practice. It's essential to be sceptical of one's own subjective experience. That's how one removes bias.

Making Science Intimate
— Roger Malina

Drawn from transcripts of a talk given at the Origins III symposium,
Ars Electronica 2011

I'm an astronomer. My original training was in physics and optics.
My background is instrument building, designing new kinds of
X-ray telescopes.

Today, we have an amazingly coherent description of the
evolution of the universe, the Concordance Model, by which we
can map the structure of the universe from the Big Bang to today.
It's a model that has great predictive power and explanatory
power. Unfortunately, for that model to work, 95% of that universe
is of an unknown nature. It is dark matter and dark energy.
It doesn't emit light and it doesn't reflect light. We only know it
exists through its gravitational effects. As an astronomer, this
is humbling. It means that after a thousand years of looking at
the sky, and building all those instruments, we understand about
3% of it. The Millennium Simulation allows us to look in detail at the
structure of the dark matter. It shows filaments of dark matter;
where they meet are where we believe black holes and galaxies
are formed. Our own galaxy is probably one of those nodes.
We don't know what dark matter is but it seems to determine the
structure and evolution of the universe. We are the decoration
in the universe – the matter that we're made of. As an astronomer,
I'm incredibly proud of the achievements of my discipline but at
the same time incredibly humble that we know almost nothing
about the most important things about the world that we live in.

The conclusion that I draw is that we are really badly designed
to understand the universe. If we want to understand quantum
mechanics, we ought to have been built on a different scale.
If we want to understand galaxies, we're built on the wrong scale
because there are different forces at play. I think this may be
one of the reasons for the disconnection of modern science and
public understanding. The information I study as a scientist is
nearly all mediated through scientific instruments. I can tell when
my instrument is hallucinating. I develop new words to describe
phenomena I encounter. I can manipulate concepts not grounded
in my experience as a child. But this intimacy is not the daily
experience of most people.

Everything about the way we think - our intuition, languages,
metaphors, arts – are all built on the wrong data to understand
the universe. There are very deep cultural and philosophical
issues that come to bear here as more and more science comes
to us through mediated data. When we talk about the impact we're
having on our planet, our senses are no good to tell us what our
impact is on our planet.

There are interesting developments in the arts that start to
address these disconnections. Artists are collecting data about
their world using technological instruments but for cultural
purposes, making powerful art and help to make science intimate,

sensual, intuitive. There are also encouraging signs of new types of "micro science" made possible by the Internet and the new public access to scientific data and instruments.

I think there are two categories of argument for why artists and scientists should work together and, indeed, why I think science agencies should fund the work of artists.

First, I think you can do better science that way. There is a huge literature on this now - on creativity arguments, innovation arguments, invention arguments. Statistically, the most successful scientists in the world engage in various kinds of artistic and cultural activity. Very deeply, they need to recontextualise their science work, and very often this takes the form of artistic and cultural activities.

Second, it leads to different science by embedding science in the larger society. I think society needs to peer review science and in order to do that you need to embed science differently in society, and that means cultural embedding and appropriation. Helga Nowotny at the European Research Council calls this "socially robust science".

This different science comes because of the "ethics of curiosity". Scientists like to say that curiosity is childlike, it's neutral, it goes into the world like a child. Bullshit. Curiosity is not neutral. As a scientist, I went to MIT and Berkley and here's what I was taught about the ethos of scientific curiosity: intellectual honesty (don't make up data), integrity (don't cheat), epistemic communism (share your data and your ideas), organised skepticism (don't believe what people tell you until it's been checked by others), dis-interestedness (don't let the company that funded your research determine the outcome of your research), impersonality (no cult of the Nobel Prize winner), and universality (what you discover in one place is valid in another). Those are the belief systems of most scientists. And there is a fundamental flaw to that. The trouble is that curiosity is embodied. You cannot make it into a neutral ideal of scientific curiosity. As Francisco Varela says: "All knowledge is conditioned by the structure of the knower".

I believe that there is an intimate relationship between what we know (and can know) and the way we're organised. To know something new, you have to change yourself. Building instruments such as the Large Hadron Collider at CERN is an act of self-construction. Curiosity drives us to change ourselves and the way we mobilise ourselves in the world. I think we underestimate very deeply how our experience impacts our ontology and epistemology. It is difficult to imagine things you haven't experienced, and there's something about experience that shapes the kinds of ideas you can have. As Sundar Sarukkai has said, curiosity is embodied, it is enacted, it's cultural, its social, it's collective.[1] And so artistic and scientific curiosities have overlapping but not identical curiosities. They drive research in different directions. Art and science have different value systems, and one of the reasons to have the arts and sciences work together is to exploit those differences.

48

1   Sundar Sarukkai is a philosopher based in Bengaluru, India

Art and science are epistemologically different terrains. We don't want to merge those terrains. We want to find ways for them to work together.

To understand the world, we have to move outside the circle of our own scales of space and time. We've only just begun to explore outside that circle. We have no proof that the scientific models we have today are a unique solution to explaining the world. They may be only one of many possible sciences that may develop in the future.

There are certain problems in our society today that are so tough that we need to change our culture to resolve them. Climate change, for example. We've got to couple science and technology to the way we live. That's a cultural problem, and we need artists working on that with the scientists every day of the next decade, the next century - if we survive it.

There are certain problems where we cannot cloister the scientific activity in the scientific world and we need to break the model. I wish that CERN, when they were discussing the risks of the Large Hadron Collider, had done so in an open societal context, not just within the CERN context.

We live in dangerous times and it's important that we find new ways to couple science to society. Part of that is having artists and scientists working together, whether that's the large-scale MIT Lab or smaller places like Arts Catalyst and SymbioticA. We need mobile, aggressive, reactive ways of creating these new approaches.

Celestial Encounters — *Nahum*

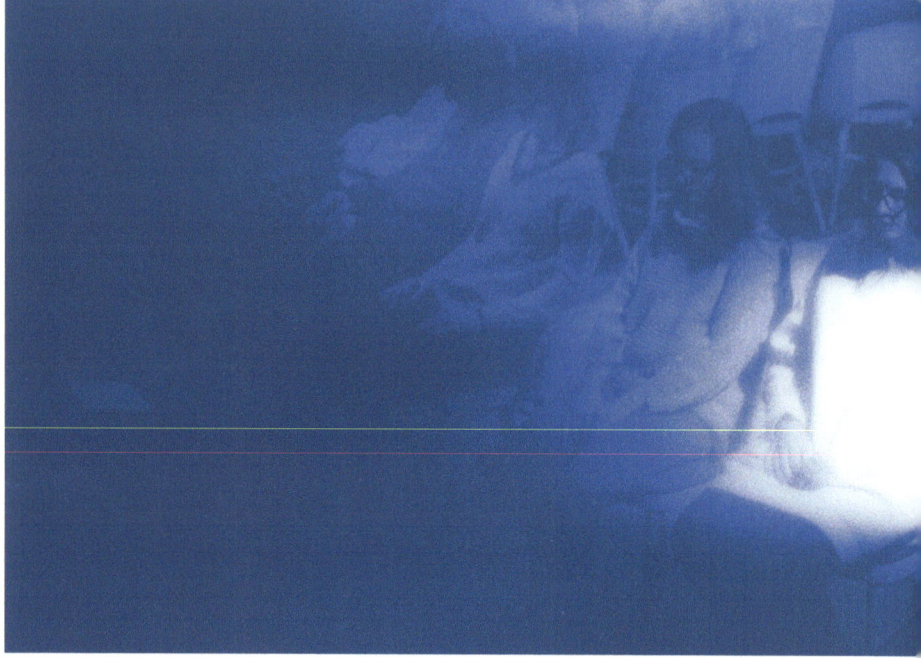

Your cooperation with this text is fundamental. I need your absolute attention to achieve a comfortable state of trance. You have a unique journey ahead and I want you to have plenty of trust in this experience. Can we do it?

You will be calm and, at all times, you will be in control of your own experience. Remember: this is for you. So please, sit comfortably as you hold this text in front of you and rest both feet on the floor.

Let's begin...
I want you to take three deep breaths.

Now breathe in ... hold it ... breathe out, and as you do allow the tension of your body to flow out.

Again, breathe in ... and now hold it for some seconds ... now breathe out. As that warm breath leaves your mouth you start feeling more and more relaxed. Please do it again.

Once more. Breathe in ... hold it ... breathe out allowing your shoulders to drop as you exhale.

Keep breathing in and out as deeply as you can. Now you can allow yourself to go into a tranquil state of trance. I would like you to stay in this place for some time, and from now on just continue breathing.

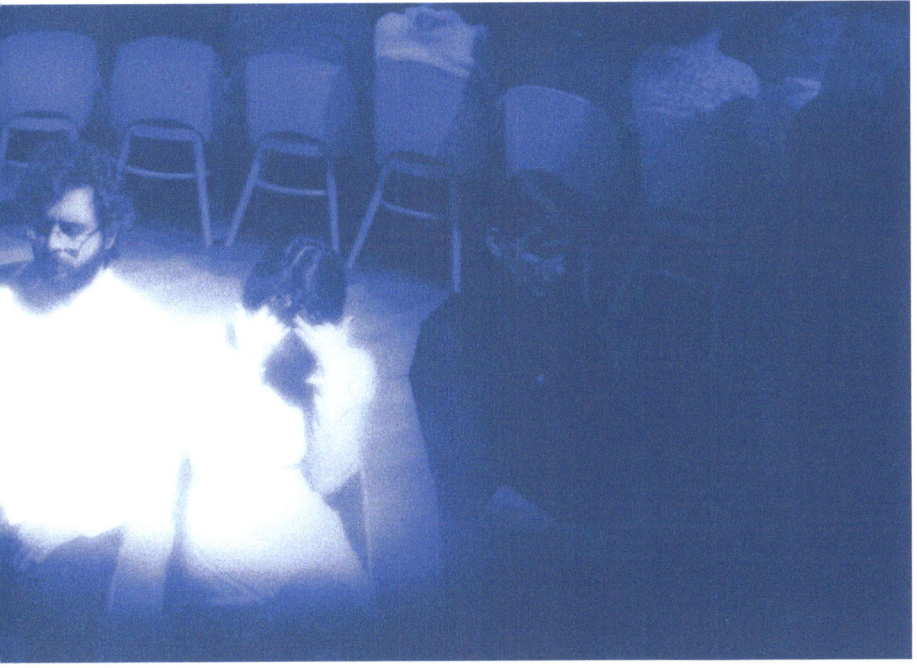

As you are sitting there, you are feeling deeply rested and you are ready to unfold an invisible face of existence.

As you read through this text, continue inhaling and exhaling as deeply as you can. I want you to gain awareness of the totality of your body, its materiality and its physical reality.

Grow aware of your head, the sensations on your face, going down to your neck and shoulders. Feel your chest as you breathe, feel your back. Feel the pressure of being seated, of your weight, and of your legs and feet. You are now conscious of your entire body.

Now I want you to concentrate on all the physical sensations. Remember that you can feel anything on your skin to a millimeter scale.

What can you feel?
The environment's temperature? The flow of air? The clothes you wear?

As you pay close attention to your entire body, I want you to zoom into these sensations. Pick any one of them and focus on it. Whatever that part of your skin is experiencing you will sense it in great detail.

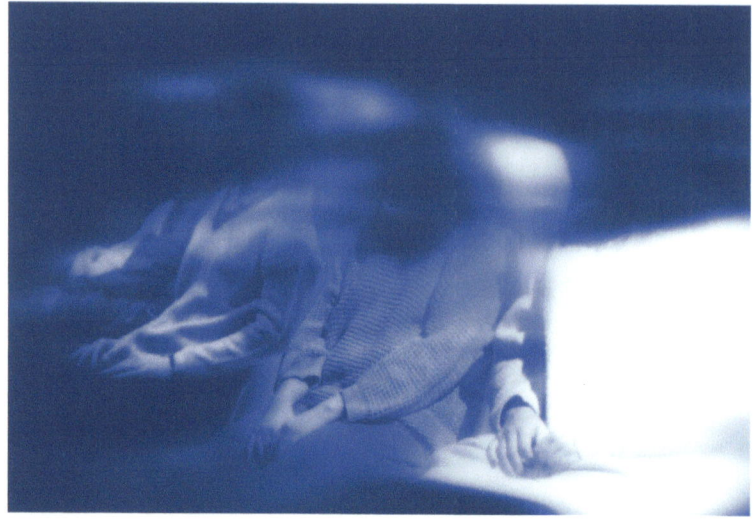

Keep zooming in as much as you can. More ... zoom in until you reach the cellular level. Go even further ... Keep going.

Deeper and deeper.

Pay all your attention to this specific point. What can you feel there? Let's try to feel further.

On that precise spot, there are other things happening and you are going to experience them. As you keep reading these words, every second there are billions and billions of minuscule particles crossing that place of your body. You haven't been aware of them until now. As you pay closer attention you gradually start to sense them.

These visitors are travelling incredibly fast and your skin isn't stopping them. They are passing straight through your body. Can you feel them?

You are sensing them. It's happening now. What can you feel?

Now that you are aware of these particles, you realise that they are coming mostly from one direction. They come from a place that provides us with warmth: the Sun. Even if it is after sunset, it makes no difference - they have passed straight through the planet almost without a trace.

Others, though, have come from even more remote sources in the universe: from supernova explosions in distant galaxies.

In their journey through boundless distances they have found you. After they pass through your skin they continue their journey straight through your tissue, your muscles and your bones, and then on. As this happens you start to imagine a picture of these encounters between you and them.

Picture how they are shooting straight through you right now. They are relentless and finally you can feel them. There are trillions. Can you see them? You are part of this extended atmosphere of the Sun.

Now this experience is part of you and you will remember it. On an intimate and physical level you are welcoming visitors from the Sun and the universe at all times. In their journeys, they have come across you, and you are now one of the many unique celestial bodies they salute on their tireless paths.

These encounters are fleeting and unlikely, just as all our other encounters in life.

Today, you have witnessed a rare perspective of your materiality and of your existence. Things change from how you think they are when you alter your perspective. You will make sure to remember this journey and, in a moment, you are going to be back to your normal self.

Let's count from one to five, and when we reach five, you will be fully awake and your everyday way of experiencing things will be reestablished.

Let's get ready: one ... two ... three ... You are waking up. Four, you are still relaxed and ready to come back from the journey. Five. You are completely awake and feeling well and calmedrelaxed. Now you can move your eyes around, move your body and start stretching.

Welcome back to the human scale.

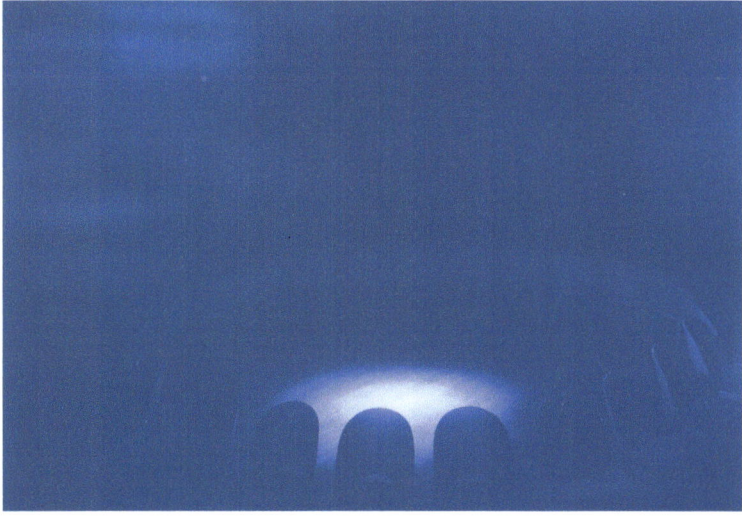

Folding a Tactile Cosmos: cosmic origami and spiderwebs — *Mark Neyrinck*

About five years ago, I went to a stunning colloquium by origamist and former physicist, Robert Lang. His work includes designing solar panels for a NASA spacecraft that could unfold. He discussed origami and its beautiful mathematics. I had been working on a geometrical method of detecting structures in computer simulations of structure formation in the universe, and I wondered: what could we learn by thinking about cosmic structures in origami terms?

It is rare that an artistic medium links conceptually so closely to a physical process. We think that something called the "dark-matter sheet" really does fold up to build structures in the cosmos. The folding operations happen in an unhelpfully abstract position-velocity phase space, but concrete, clarifying origami concepts still apply to the folded-up structure if the abstract velocity coordinates are squashed flat. Knowledge has increased in both directions: from science to origami, and from origami to science. It is especially valuable for tactile understanding, which is usually absent in astronomy. I recall a professional meeting where I handed out origami to fold - this was the only point of the conference where all attendees were fully engaged, not a single laptop out.

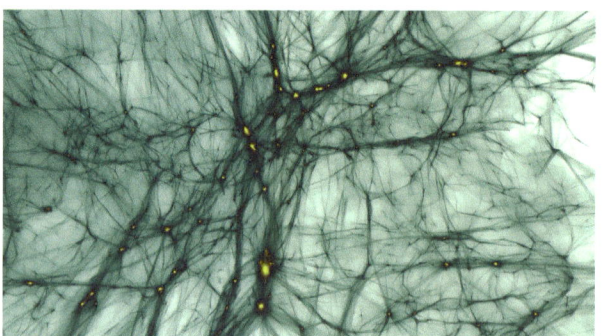

Origami ideas of folding "dark matter sheet" enabled this rendering by Ralf Kähler. Courtesy Ralf Kahler (KPIAC/SLAC/Stanford). Simulation by Oliver Hahn and Tom Abel

Scientifically, this origami view has led to my toy "origami" approximation of the large-scale arrangement of matter in the universe, which helps to explain, for example, why matter filaments typically extend from galaxies and why nearby galaxies connected by filaments tend to rotate in a similar direction.[1]

Recently, I designed an origami tessellation from a patch of the VIPERS galaxy survey. Students and I folded it in an "Origami

---

1 Mark C. Neyrinck, "Tetrahedral collapse: a rotational toy model of simultaneous dark-matter halo, filament and wall formation", *Monthly Notices of the Royal Astronomical Society* 460, no. 1 (2016): 816-826.

Mathematics and Cosmology" short course at Johns Hopkins. It was deeply engaging for everyone involved. In the middle panel below, tiny white dots show the raw locations of galaxies in the survey. The yellow lines are crease lines, showing where to fold the pattern.

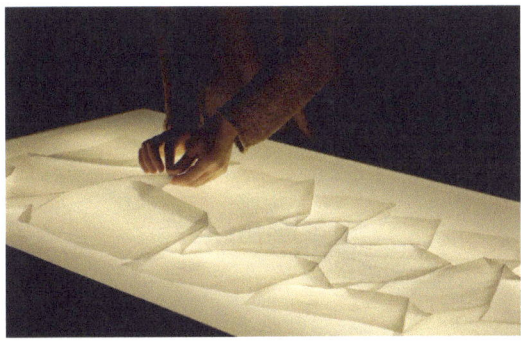

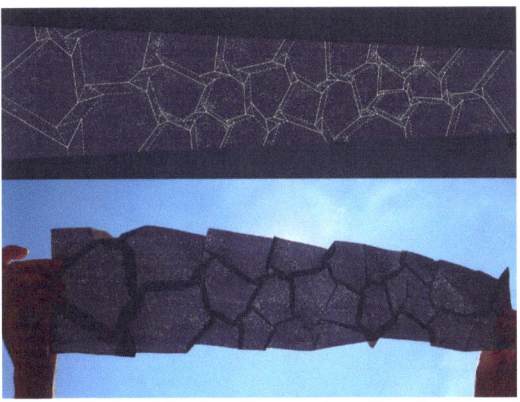

Origami representations of the VIPERS survey, http://vipers.inaf.it, by the author and students in the 2015 "Origami Mathematics and Cosmology" course at JHU. Top panel photographed by Ben Andrew

These designs are based on a vast patch of the universe billions of light-years away, but the next design focuses on the close-to-home "Council of Giants",[2] our nearest dozen or so galaxies that happen to be in a flat arrangement. Robert Lang has written about the correspondence between origami tessellations and "spiderwebs", i.e. spatial networks of threads that can be strung up entirely in tension.[3] This led to our recent paper exploring the

2   Marshall L McCall, "A Council of Giants", *Monthly Notices of the Royal Astronomical Society* 440, no. 1 (2014): 405-426.

3   Robert J Lang, A. Bateman, "Every spider web has a simple flat twist tessellation" in Origami⁵: *Fifth International Meeting of Origami Science, Mathematics, and Education*, eds. P Wang-Iverson, RJ Lang, Y Mark (2011): 455–473; Robert J Lang, "Spiderwebs, Tilings, and Flagstone Tessellations" in *Origami⁶: I. Mathematics* (2015): 189; Robert J Lang, *Twists, Tilings, and Tessellations: Mathematical Methods for Geometric Origami* (CRC Press 2018)

shared geometry of these networks.[4] Here are my approximate origami and dreamcatcher (spider web) representations of this Council of Giants.

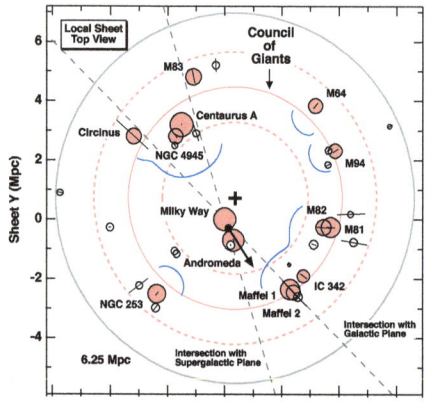

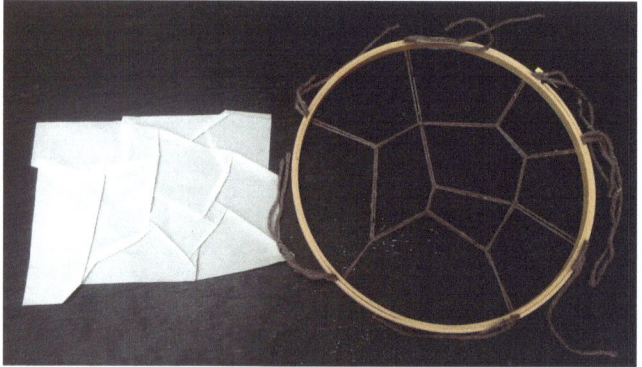

Scientific, origami and dreamcatcher/spiderweb views
of the Council of Giants

The correspondence between origami tessellations, spiderwebs, and the cosmic web gives a rigorous underpinning to the observation that the cosmic web is spiderweb-like, made by artists (e.g. Tomás Saraceno[5]), scientists,[6] and journalists. Practically in astronomy, this correspondence could be of use to correct galaxy distances in galaxy surveys, to match these networks' geometry.

Concepts related to folding can help to understand a lot in nature, beyond cosmology. The study of projections of folded forms is essentially catastrophe theory, which explains some non-intuitive effects in a wide variety of fields, from stock market

4   Mark C. Neyrinck, Johan Hidding, Marina Konstantatou, and Rien van de Weygaert, "The cosmic spiderweb: equivalence of cosmic, architectural, and origami tessellations", submitted to Roy Soc Open Science (2018), arXiv:1710.04509
5   Philip Ball, "World of webs", *Nature* 543 (2017): 314–314.
6   Mario Livio, "From Spider Webs to the Cosmic Web", Huffington Post (2012); Benedikt Diemer and Isaac Facio, "The Fabric of the Universe: Exploring the Cosmic Web in 3D Prints and Woven Textiles", *Pubs. Astr. Soc. Pacific* 129, 058013 (2017).

crashes to light playing on the bottom of a swimming pool.
I was talking about spiderwebs and origami to Allan McRobie,
a Cambridge structural engineer and an expert on spider web-like
structures. He has been looking at catastrophe theory and folding
in art and drawing.[7] Whereas the cosmic web described in the
"origami spider web" is entirely angular, his work on catastrophe
theory is all about smooth curves - the angular spider web is
only an approximation to the reality. Both perspectives help to
understand the structure.

This wonderful conversation reminded me that all we have
to understand the universe is our artistic mind, which cannot
grasp the universe in its raw, entirely objective form. To know
the universe and how we occupy it as well as possible requires
multiple ways of viewing, most of which involve art.

Bibliography

Ball, Philip, "World of webs", Nature 543 (2017): 314–314.
Diemer, Benedikt, and Isaac Facio, "The Fabric of the Universe:
Exploring the Cosmic Web in 3D Prints and Woven Textiles", *Pubs.
Astr. Soc. Pacific* 129, 058013 (2017), arXiv:1702.03897.
Gjerde, Eric, *Origami tessellations: awe-inspiring geometric
designs* (Boca Raton: CRC Press, 2009).
Lang, Robert J and A. Bateman, "Every spider web has a simple
flat twist tessellation" in Origami[5]: *Fifth International Meeting
of Origami Science, Mathematics, and Education*, eds. P Wang-
Iverson, RJ Lang, Y Mark (2011): 455–473.
Lang, Robert J, "Spiderwebs, Tilings, and Flagstone Tessellations"
in Origami[6]: *Sixth International Meeting of Origami Science,
Mathematics*, eds. Miura K, Kawasaki T, Tachi T, Uehara R, Lang RJ,
Wang-Iverson P, American Mathematical Soc. (2015): 189.
Lang, Robert J, *Twists, Tilings, and Tessellations: Mathematical
Methods for Geometric Origami* (CRC Press 2018)
Livio, Mario, "From Spider Webs to the Cosmic Web", Huffington
Post (2012), http://www.huffingtonpost.com/mario-livio/from-
spider-webs-to-the-cosmic-web_b_1594086.html
McRobie, Allan, *The seduction of curves: the lines of beauty that
connect mathematics, art, and the nude* (Princeton: Princeton
University Press, 2017)
McCall, Marshall L., "A Council of Giants", *Monthly Notices of the
Royal Astronomical Society* 440, no. 1 (2014): 405-426.
Neyrinck, Mark C., "Tetrahedral collapse: a rotational toy
model of simultaneous dark-matter halo, filament and wall
formation", *Monthly Notices of the Royal Astronomical Society* 460,
no. 1 (2016): 816-826.
Neyrinck, Mark C., Johan Hidding, Marina Konstantatou, and Rien
van de Weygaert, "The cosmic spiderweb: equivalence of cosmic,
architectural, and origami tessellations", submitted to Roy Soc
Open Science (2018), arXiv:1710.04509

---

7   Allan McRobie, *The seduction of curves: the lines of beauty that connect
    mathematics, art, and the nude* (Princeton: Princeton University Press, 2017)

58

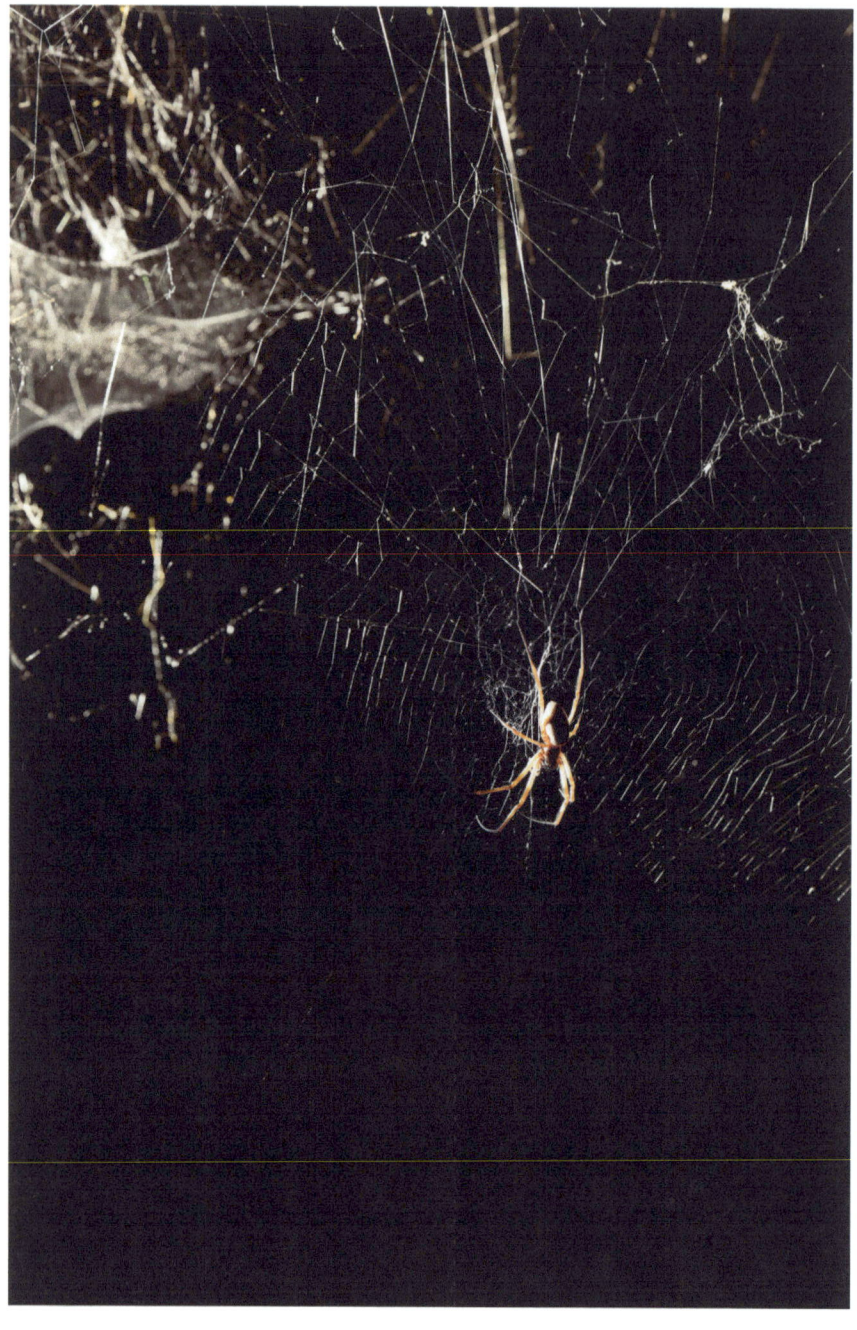

Tomás Saraceno, *Hyperweb of the Present*, 2017
Installation at the 14th Lyon Biennial Floating Worlds, curated by Emma Lavigne.
Courtesy the artist, Andersen's Contemporary, Copenhagen, Ruth Benzacar,
Buenos Aires, Tanya Bonakdar Gallery, New York, Pinksummer Contemporary Art,
Genoa, Esther Schipper, Berlin.
Photography © see pictures
(pp 17, 58, 60-61)

Hyperweb of the Present
— *Tomás Saraceno*

[...] space by itself, and time by itself, are doomed to fade away into mere shadows, and only a kind of union of the two will preserve an independent reality.

Thus physicist Hermann Minkowski began his speech in the 80th Assembly of German Natural Scientists and Physicians in 1908. For Minkowski, space (volume) and time (duration) alone were not enough to define reality and objects. He called for unity between the three dimensions of space (height, length and width) and the fourth dimension of time, calling this simply "the World". Minkowski's famous light cone diagram serves as one of the models that graphically explain the reality of spacetime.

The artwork *Hyperweb of the Present* is an artistic appropriation of the hypersurface of the present – an element in Minkowski's diagram. As in his theoretical drawing, two light cones centered on a point named an event - the instantaneous physical situation or occurrence associated with a point in spacetime. One light ray illuminates a frame holding a suspended hybrid spider web[1] with a living arachnea (spider) sitting inside and vibrating the web. The second light ray projects part of another work by Saraceno, a video piece of tampered temporalities, 163,000 light years[2]. It screens the image of the Large Magellanic Cloud, a galaxy visible from the Southern Hemisphere. The light emitted from this galaxy takes 163,000 years to reach the Earth's surface. It illuminates the hybrid web in a pale blue hue. The vibrations of a living spider are recorded with a set of microphones and amplified to make the installation's soundtrack.

Hyperweb of the Present is a space that symbolises an event now and here in ontological-physical terms. Minkowski tells that the present moment or the real is a grain in the universe where two light cones, the one of the past and the one of the future meet. Through the installation we look at this event, and find the tiny universe of a spider, or the World. The past and the future light cones meet where we cast our gaze and where the spider exists in that specific moment; a hyperweb of present entanglements floating suspended.

1 A Hybrid Web (or a Hybrid Spider Web - HSW) is a spider web cluster envisioned and designed by Tomás Saraceno, in which two or more different spiders from different species weave webs in the same space, using the architecture of each other's webs to form a complex, hybrid structure.

2 *163,000 Light Years*, a film by Tomás Saraceno, lasts 163,000 years, the length of time that it takes for the light that is traveling through space, to reach the Earth. What one sees in the film, as in the sky, is always the past. It is actually the light that was emitted from the Large Magellanic Cloud 163,000 years ago... We, earthlings, are always convicted to watch the past...

Tomás Saraceno, *Hyperweb of the Present*, 2017
The abstract soundtrack of *163,00 Light Years*, a film by Tomás
Saraceno, which forms part of the work, comes from the collision of
two large black-holes, 1.3 billion years ago, now projected on Earth.
Spacetime is not a fixed construction, but rather an action that could,
speculatively, warp the length of the film before its end. Similar to the
waves that animate the surface of the salt flats in Uyuni, Bolivia, where
the film was shot, gravitational waves ripple spacetime in waxing and
waning movements, twisting a linear conception of time. Different
temporalities appear, dimensions are projected and epochs redefined.

60

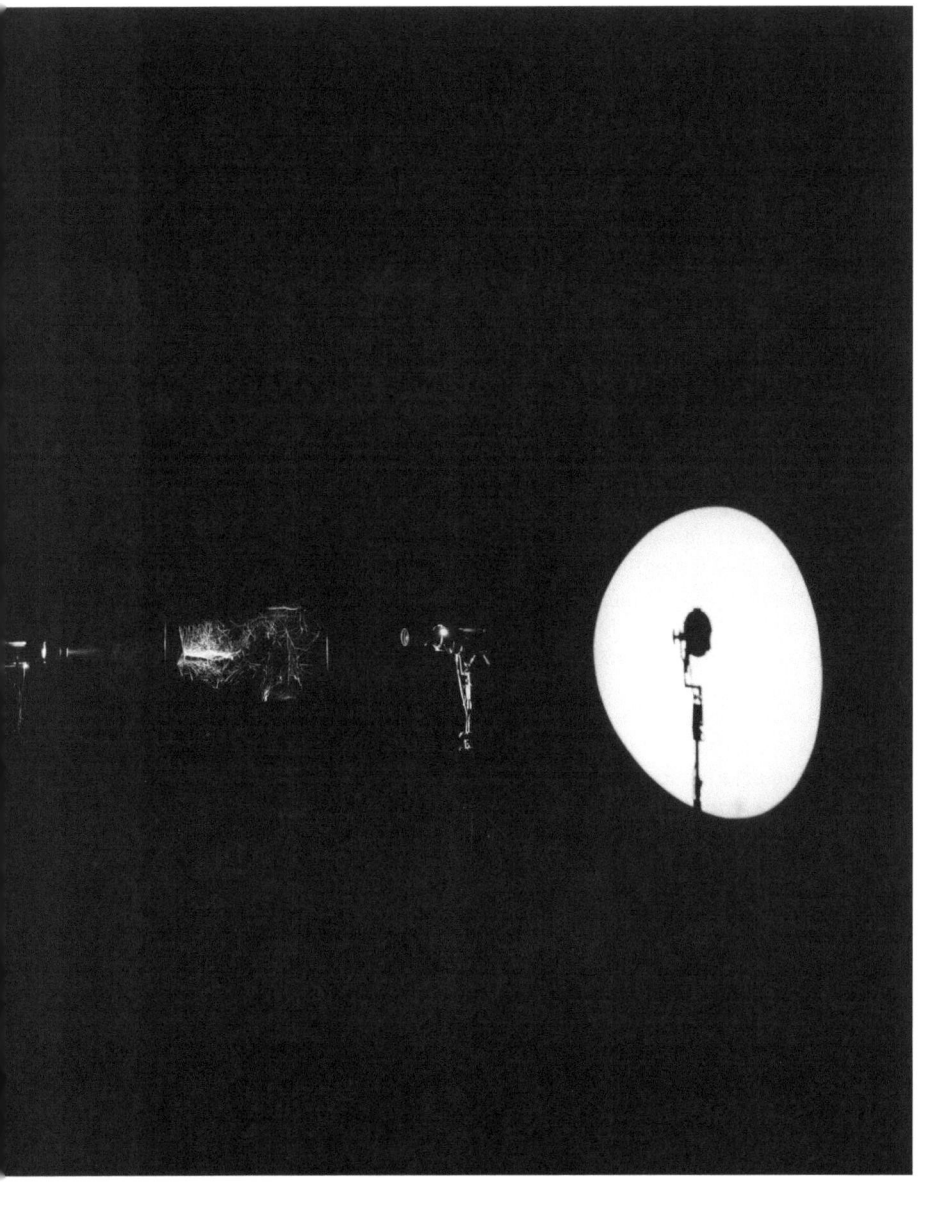

Physics through the Lens of Dance
— *Flaviu Cipcigan*

Dance is a beautiful way of expression. Through dance, we learn about our bodies and our minds. We express feelings, we connect with others, and create art in motion. It's no wonder that dancing is being investigated as effective exercise, therapy and communication.

In this essay, I want to explore another, less visible facet of dancing: the nature of knowledge expressed by dance and how this connects with my scientific practice.

A fundamental aspect of science is the process of acquiring, encoding, and communicating knowledge. From the roots of science in natural philosophy, knowledge is mainly written, as words or as mathematical symbols. A book uses words to describe rich sensations, and the connections between them: movement, sights, sounds, smells, feelings. Saying "I jumped with joy when I heard her footsteps" describes a complex sensation that you can understand only once experienced.

This form of knowledge has enhanced our natural capabilities to a point where our imagination rather than our capability is the limit to what we can create. We can predict the motion of planets, fly over the Atlantic Ocean, communicate instantly over vast distances, and learn as much as our curiosity and time allows.

But, this form of knowledge expresses a very limited set of human capabilities. We perform most of our intellectual activities while sitting. As I type these words, I am stretching my mind, yet keeping my body rigid.

Dance is rich in body expression, stretching our bodies and our minds. In tango, small movements of the chest of a leader communicate intention to the follower. Small movements in her body communicate a response. Every time I embrace someone, I start a conversation and a process of acquiring knowledge. How does my body move today? How do you respond to what I say through my movements? Just like a language, this connection requires years of practice to learn and a lifetime of mastering. However, once learned, this body language leads to a way of acquiring knowledge that is intimate and embodied.

How would science look like through this lens of intimate, embodied knowledge? To illustrate this, let's start with a recent research about the motion of bees. Research suggests that bees detect flowers by the electric field they give. As a charged balloon makes your hair stand on one end, the electric field of flowers brushes against the little hairs on a bee's body, alerting her of a flower nearby. As we enhanced our minds to understand the motion of planets, can we enhance our bodies to experience a bee's tug?

Art provides us with a way to do so: Micol Assaël's *Chizhevsky Lessons*. In this installation, charged copper panels fill a room with static electricity. Entering the room, the hairs on your arms would start to tingle, followed by your skin and the rest of your body. Standing in the room, you would literally feel the electricity.

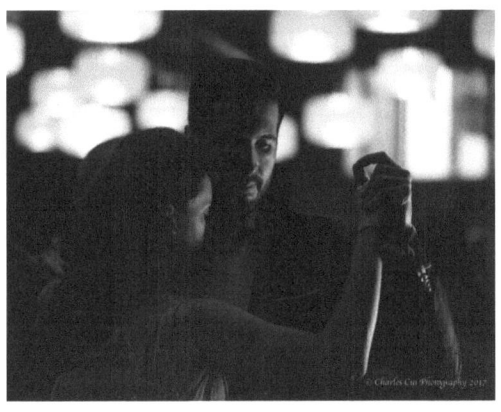

The author dancing. Photo: Charles Cui

Imagine a similar installation. A black room, lights turned off. You enter and stand motionless for a few minutes to allow your mind to tune to your body. As you step, your hair starts to tingle. Parts of the room are filled with static, forming trails of electricity that guide you and invite you to follow them. As you walk, the sensation gets more powerful until you reach a glass sphere placed on a tall pedestal. When you get close, the sphere will start shining, together with the path you were just on. The light will then fade, being replaced by another river of electricity for you to follow.

Such an installation would not only be a unique physical experience, but will give you intimate and physical knowledge about a part of nature: how bees find flowers. Reading the sentence "bees are attracted by the electric fields of flowers" is as different to the real experience of bees as reading the sentence "I jumped with joy" is different to the actual feeling of joy. A space such as the one described here allows you to experience the meaning behind abstract information, not as ink on a paper or pixels on a screen, but as the very architecture of the building intimately interacting with your body.

Seymour Papert's "Literacy and Letteracy in the Media Ages" discusses this expansion of knowledge from something in our head to an environment we can interact with. His "knowledge machine" is a place where a child, before being able to read, can nonetheless experience being with giraffes in Africa and understand how they sleep, through images, sounds, smells and feelings. Literacy would then stop being the ability to read, but the ability to interact with knowledge expressed in this Knowledge Machine. People will then put equal effort in being able to speak a language as being able to speak a body language.

The idea of a knowledge space that involves and addresses all our senses is becoming more and more relevant in today's world. We gather large quantities of data about our environment and about ourselves: from our shopping habits, to our movement and the rhythm of our hearts. Making sense of this data doesn't only require clever algorithms. It requires new ways of representing knowledge, ways that engage all our senses, are intimate and sensual, rather than disconnect us further from our bodies.

Central Engine Maintenance Perfomance
— *Annie Carpenter*

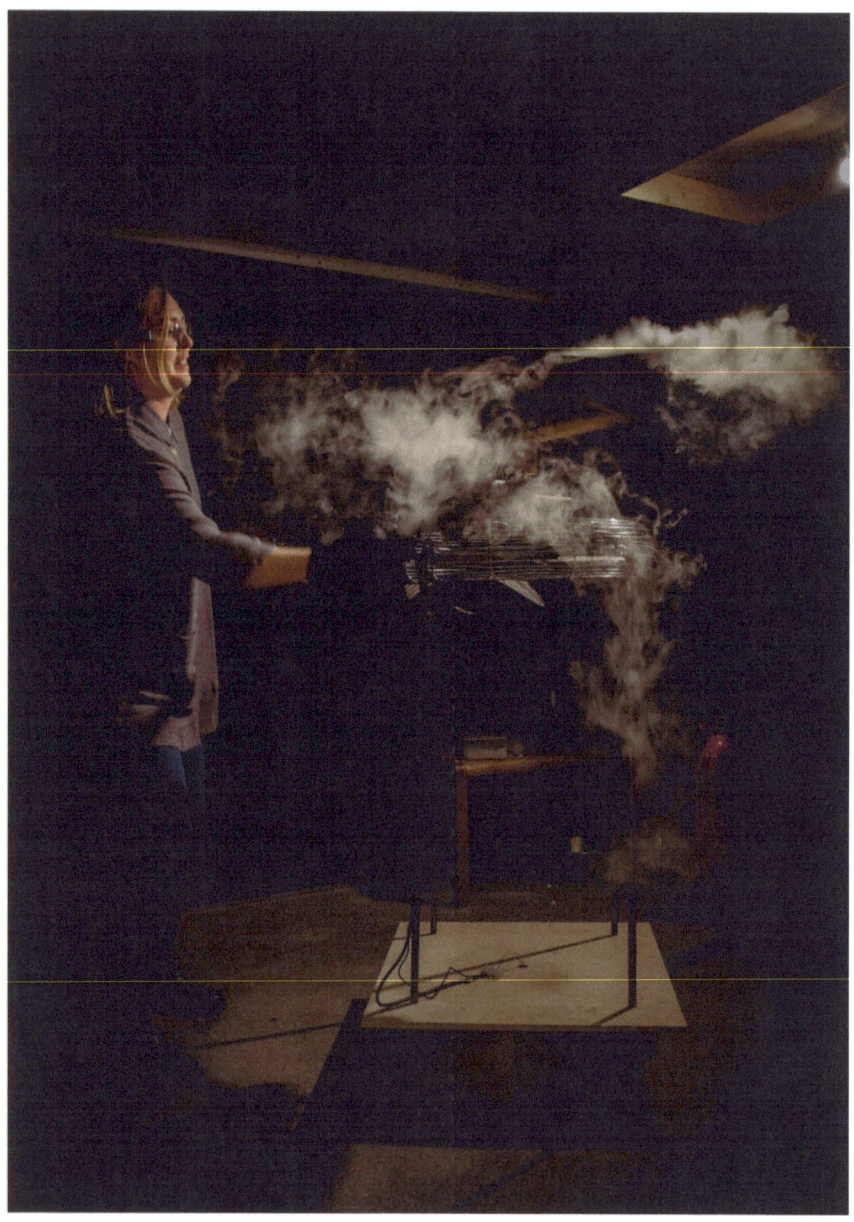

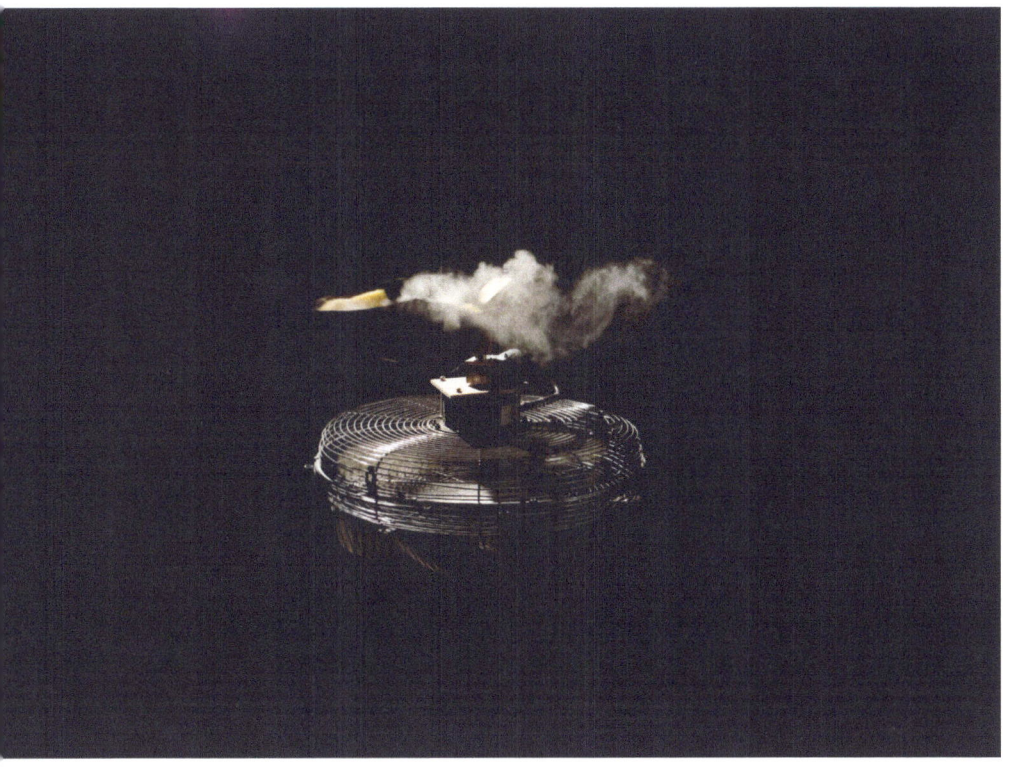

Central Engine attempts to model a black hole accretion disk.
The sculpture is activated by a 'maintenance performance' in
which CO2 is released from a fire extinguisher to produce dry
ice. This creates the fog which pours from the orbiting vessel and
curves into the spinning fan. The piece is influenced by an interest
in the spaces where scientific knowledge starts to break down:
fluid dynamics around black holes can currently only be guessed
at due to the vast distances involved.

Annie Carpenter, *Central Engine Maintenance Performance*, 2016
Commissioned by Castlefield Gallery for the exhibition 'Miniature World',
Kinetic sculpture and demonstration; welded steel, fan, brass vessel, motor, dry ice
Photographs: John Lynch

Life is Astronomical — *Marek Kukula*

In 1610, Galileo Galilei's pamphlet *The Starry Messenger* became the talk of Europe, with its description of what could be seen in the heavens through the newly-invented telescope. Galileo's use of observation, evidence and reasoning to support the Copernican model, in which the Earth was no longer the centre of the cosmos, was correctly understood by many readers as a challenge, not just to cosy beliefs about humanity's place in the universe, but to the basis of religious and secular authority itself. But Galileo's discoveries were conveyed to the world not only by his words but also by his skill as an artist. In the sixteenth and seventeenth centuries, the subjects that we now call science were considered part and parcel of a humanist education. Galileo himself lectured on both mathematics and art theory, and was known for his skill in chiaroscuro - a discipline that he put to good use in his exquisite depictions of the shadowy mountains and craters of the Moon (which received wisdom had held to be smooth and featureless).

Perhaps unsurprisingly for a science based on observation, the relationship between astronomy and art is a long one. In the late eighteenth century, the society portrait painter John Russell led a double life as an amateur astronomer. His delicate pastel "portraits" of the Moon, one of which is in the collection of the Royal Observatory at Greenwich, capture colour and texture as well as cartographic detail. They were a part of a life-long fascination that led Russell to produce the Selenographia (also now in the Greenwich collection), an astonishingly sophisticated scientific instrument in the form of a lunar globe that simulates the Moon's complex motions as well as its topography. Russell's contemporaries William and Caroline Herschel also had careers that combined art and science, starting as successful musicians and carving out reputations as two of the best-known astronomers of the period.

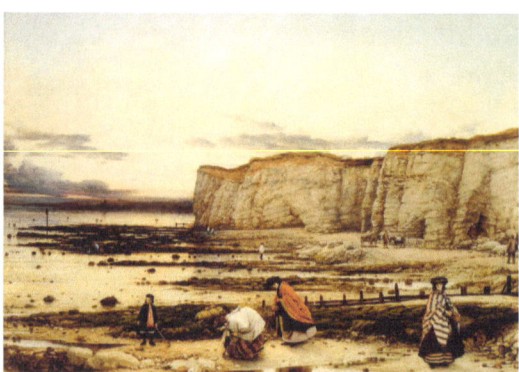

William Dyce, *Pegwell Bay, Kent - a Recollection of October 5th 1858*, ?1858-60, courtesy of Tate

In the twenty first century, scientists and their institutions increasingly see artists as powerful allies for engaging the public with science. But it would be a mistake to think of art in instrumental terms, solely as a vehicle for education and PR.

In William Dyce's Pre-Raphaelite painting *Pegwell Bay, Kent - a Recollection of October 5th 1858* (now in Tate Britain), the artist depicts members of his family hunting for seashells on a beach. The inclusion of the date in the painting's title and the specifics of the scene – low tide, sunset – conjure a very particular moment in time. And yet the chalk cliffs in the background and the barely visible ghostly apparition of Donati's Comet in the evening sky provide a disquieting counterpoint to the record of a family daytrip to the seaside. By the mid nineteenth century, scientific discoveries about the age of the Earth and the scale of the cosmos were again challenging long-held beliefs about humanity's significance. The chalk of the cliffs was known to have been laid down on the bed of a long-vanished sea millions of years in the past, while the comet, which had attained its maximum brightness on the date of the title, would not return until thousands of years in the future. The devout Dyce perhaps intended to set the eternal and limitless extent of God's power against the tiny compass of the human lifespan. But for many of his contemporaries the overwhelming timescales and unthinkable distances revealed by geology and astronomy - the disciplines that Tennyson dubbed the "Dark Muses" - were deeply unsettling. There is ambiguity too in the obsessively photorealistic style of the picture. Painted in 1859-60, this is not, despite appearances, an accurate record made on the spot, but a "recollection", perhaps altered by time and possibly combining elements from different memories to create a coherent whole. Whatever Dyce's original intent, his artwork poses some very modern questions about the place of humanity in an immense and ancient cosmos and about the role of memory and objectivity in our interpretation of it.

In the work of many contemporary artists, we see the same ability to provide surprising perspectives, explore philosophical implications and make connections between scientific concepts and lived experience. Like Dyce's painting, Wolfgang Tillmans' work also interrogates our assumptions about truth and evidence, and by placing astronomical photographs side by side with diverse and varied views of Earth-bound life, Tillmans makes a powerful point that human culture is itself a cosmological phenomenon. In the words of the artist "life is astronomical".

In the seventeenth century, one of the most shocking aspects of Galileo Galilei's claims about the nature of the universe was his use of observation and experiment to challenge the received wisdom of Aristotelian philosophy. But it has been argued that this was a trait that he learned from his father, the musician and composer Vincenzo Galilei. In his *Dialogue on Ancient and Modern Music* the elder Galilei writes: "It appears to me that they who in proof of anything rely simply on the weight of authority, without adducing any argument in support of it, act very absurdly. I, on the contrary, wish to be allowed to raise questions freely and to answer without any adulation, as becomes those who are truly in search of the truth."

Space-Time Relations: rocks as a halfway point between matter and meaning
— *Harry Lawson*

I started collecting rocks as a reason for getting out of my studio and to places where I might not have otherwise have gone. My journeys took me around the UK, to Iceland, and to Passaic, New Jersey, following Robert Smithson's journey from in his essay *A tour of the New Monuments of Passaic, New Jersey*, shaping for me the idea of relics as 'monuments' and the entanglement of technology, geology and time.

After these journeys, I decided that rocks needed some meaning or reason to be in my collection. There were rocks I wanted that I couldn't get by visiting sites and I began to scour the Internet. One of the first objects I bought was a meteorite. This cosmic object's appearance was unremarkable, although it had been traveling for billions of years. It seemed bizarre that an object of this magnitude could be packaged, sold and sent to me through the post. Technological advances have changed how information is stored within materials. Information and knowledge are now stored remotely, often on far-flung servers in the ocean or isolated areas on earth. The chances of its long-term storage and retrieval in the far future becomes less likely, highlighting why so much of the knowledge we have from the distant past is only retrievable through hardy material like stone.

In the wake of buying the meteorite, I began to wonder whether an Internet 'rock' could exist and what form it would take. My collection has become an expanded idea of what a rock could be, a sort of charting of our existence, what came before us, and what will be left behind after the Earth has gone. It has become a dialogue about whether information can really travel through deep time and if it can be preserved. The brass replica of the Voyager 1 Golden Disk is one example: an object that floats through outer space and cosmic time, attempting to explain what it is, where it came from and who made it through symbols and inscriptions.

Along this path, associations between the rocks started to emerge, and display methods have become an integral way to articulate meaning within the collection. Constructing cabinets has become my way of interacting with the rocks. As the collection grows, new themes emerge, broadening my understanding of how meaning is carried within these geologic materials.

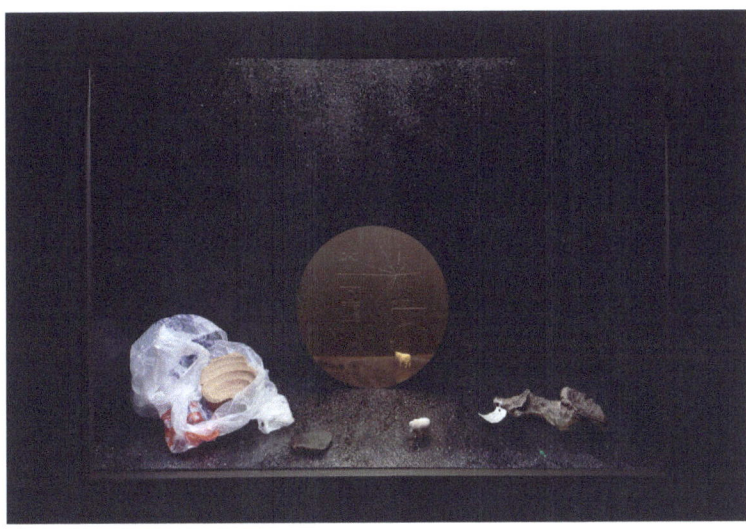

Harry Lawson, *Space + Time Relations*, 2017

Objects in the cabinet called Remote Objects/Space-Time Relations:

A replica of the golden disk on Voyager 1
Brass copy of the plate fixed to the Voyager 1 Spacecraft.
The original is nearly 200,000,000,000km from Earth.

An Egyptian pot in a Tesco's bag
A genuine, approximately 3000-year old Egyptian pot given
to me wrapped in a Tesco bag by an archaeologist friend.

A Chondrite Meteorite
Chondrite meteorites formed before any galaxies and are some
of the oldest objects in the universe. This one could be as old as
4.5 billion years.

A Netsuke of a Cow
A Japanese Netsuke carved from bone. It interested me because
it looked like a Neolithic cave drawing of a cow.

A cast of a fossil of a Tyrannosaurus Brain
When I found this object on eBay, there was nothing in the image
to give it a sense of scale. I assumed it was massive, but when it
arrived, it was less than 15cm long, making the Tyrannosaurus
not a very clever dinosaur.

The Blackboard
— *Massimo Mannarelli & Fiona Crisp*

The following is an edited extract from a filmed conversation between Massimo Mannarelli, theoretical physicist at Laboratori Nazionali del Gran Sasso, and Fiona Crisp, artist. The full conversation can be accessed at www.materialsight. wordpress.com.

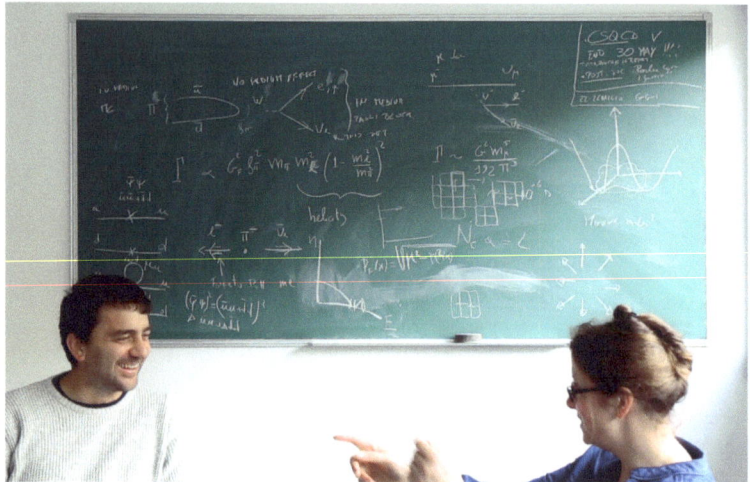

Fiona Crisp — I've been thinking, since our last conversation, about the idea of 'constructing space'. You spoke about creating scenarios or worlds that don't exist ... evolving things in mathematics that don't exist in the world. This creation of space interests me from the perspective of how I work with photography, as I'm intrigued by the idea of 'impossible space'. When I'm working, it's not a question of *what* I'm looking at but *how* I'm looking at it. What I'm trying to think about is constructing a space that is in some way impossible. The work is not a documentary image of a space. The way the camera looks at something, it constructs a space within the image that is a kind of impossibility.

You spoke about the way you are using mathematics and that sometimes you're creating things that don't actually exist ... You're able to put something in an equation that suggests something complex ... sometimes beyond your cognition?

Massimo Mannarelli — The thing is, which is somehow similar to what you said about your work, that we try to find another description of reality ... Reality is what surrounds us, but our description of reality is by means of mathematics. I like your non-documentary approach because it's close to my view that mathematics speaks by itself. The standard view is that you look at a phenomenon and then you write down an equation trying to describe it. But, in my view, what you are actually doing is deriving a theory. Then you start to explore this equation and figure out how the implications of this equation are reflected in the real world. It's not that you are really describing the world. You are

somehow exploring it by means of this incredible tool ... It's a tool
for exploration and for understanding, a deep understanding in my
opinion. Then you see whether your description via this equation
corresponds to reality, whether it matches.

Sometimes you'll find that a model that you have built doesn't
actually match with nature, or it matches only at a certain scale.
There are models that work very well for cosmology for example,
but you can never think of using them for scanning microscopic
physics or atoms ... There's a description of matter that is not
universal but can only be applied in a certain domain. And maybe
a tool doesn't completely work in a different domain .... It's like you
were saying, that you cannot take a documentary picture. I like this.

FC — It's hard for a lot of people to get their head around! This
morning we've been underground in the laboratory [at Gran
Sasso] and there's always that expectation from others that you're
documenting what this environment is. But really I'm trying to find
a way of looking at that environment to talk about its haptic or
material quality ... as well as thinking conceptually about what the
different experiments are exploring, which are extraordinary in
themselves. Earlier today we were in the Large Volume Detector,
which is one of the only experiments that I've come across here or
at other laboratories that you can walk through like architecture.
It is like a cityscape ... like New York! What is also interesting is
that the photo-multipliers are on the surface, not hidden inside.
It isn't like with other detectors, where you're looking at the outside
of a huge object knowing intellectually that these layers of photo-
multipliers are in the detector core, but unable to access them
visually.

One of the sub-texts of this research project [*Material Sight*] is
why we find it so difficult to connect to your areas of fundamental
science. We can connect to biomedical science because of our
intrinsic interest in ourselves. Even if genetics is complex, we still

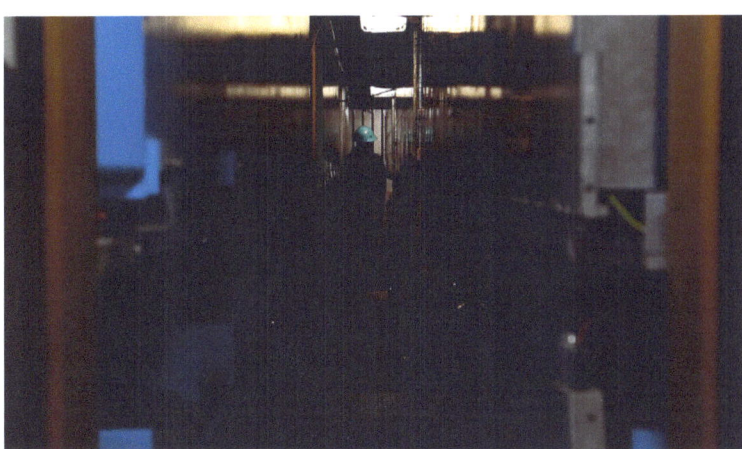

Fiona Crisp, *Large Volume Detector: Laboratori Nazionali del Gran Sasso*, 2017
Single channel video
Image courtesy the artist and Matt's Gallery, London

have an interest in it because it's about our bodies, our families and our histories. But with fundamental science, it's so removed from us - the macro-scale and the micro-scale - and we can no longer use our bodies as a measure. So it's through this, through my language, that I start to think about these spaces ...

I find this incredibly interesting, your spaces of theory and the way that you have spoken about your methodologies, but also the idea that your knowledge is also constructed through practice.

72   MM — Yes, that's fundamental. It's one of the things that you try to teach to students, which is the reason why they have to do their exercises! It's important that they understand applications, but it is also important that they try extremes. I mean, you have an equation but what happens if, in this problem, the mass goes to infinity? If the question gives you something that doesn't match your intuition, there are two possibilities. The first is that your result is wrong, and the second that your intuition doesn't work, but in most cases you've understood and learnt something.

Some people feel scared when you start thinking on large-scales - not only of mass, but of distances - or the opposite, if you go to the very small, because your intuition doesn't help you anymore. That's why at that point you only trust mathematics, because that's the only tool that we have for dealing with the scales that we don't understand ... We cannot really imagine the behaviour of particles and so on but somehow you build your map in your mind saying, "Okay, that phenomenon can be explained by this."

FC — Then you have a coordinate?

MM — Then you have a coordinate, right.

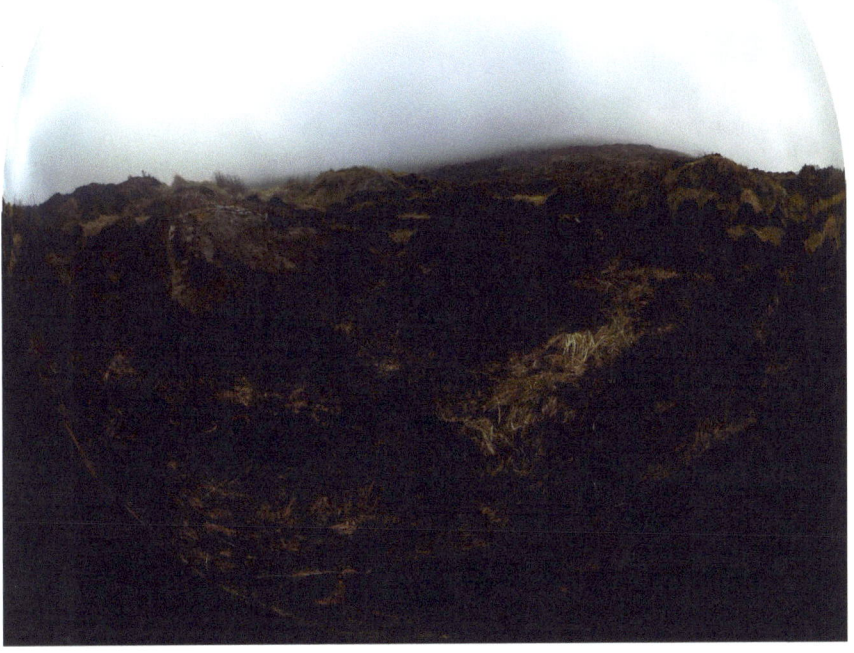

Phil Coy, *Substance, a whole history of hollows and reliefs*, 2017
Hemispheric film still

Substance, a whole history of hollows and reliefs explores the materials and processes that enable us to create images of the earth's surface, revealing the scars that the extraction of these materials leave behind. The film combines material shot at ancient copper mines in Anglesey and West Cork, as well as processes involved in the manufacture of satellites and the UK's largest Super Computer at Rutherford Appleton Laboratory (RAL Space).

The films sound score includes audio cut from interviews by leading research scientists at RAL Space: Hugh Mortimer, Erica Yang and Nick Waltham. Their combined research in the fields of computer science and remote sensor design forms an integral part of the technologies used to provide and read satellite data, and as such has a profound effect on how we view and interpret the world.

It was just a line of pixels, one line
— *Phil Coy*

how clean a process can you get?
with no muck in the system
you'll generate masks
create a mask set
grow a silicon wafer
probe it with precision light sources

invented by Boyle and Smith in nineteen-sixty-nine
the charged coupled device
small, light weight, linear
just a line of pixels, one line
by the early seventies
it was one hundred by one hundred
a largish twenty or thirty microns each

then the holy grail
build bigger and bigger charged coupled devices
the standard US Television sensor size
three-hundred and twenty, by two-hundred and fifty-six

so you're looking down at earth
trying to get a clear image
and across the whole spectral range
whilst travelling seven and half thousand kilometers per second
so you need a high frame rate
roughly one hundred and sixty micro seconds

a special stitching technique
depending upon mission requirements, ninety million pixels
shining a pattern onto a silicon wafer
a limit to the field of view
photolithography defines the structure
thousands and thousands on a single wafer
electrically test it
then saw it up

you want the dynamic range but not the noise
as you cool the silicon down
you have to care about the dark charge

Arts at CERN, fostering new cultures at the largest laboratory in the world
— *Mónica Bello*

Over recent years, various scientific institutions have nurtured novel models of dialogue and cooperation between scientists, and artists and cultural centres have increasingly been incorporating art and science explorations into their activities. Today, it is obvious that scientific engagement with cultural practices acts as an important driver for novel scenarios for knowledge exchange. At CERN, the European Organisation for Nuclear Research in Geneva, physicists and engineers are probing the fundamental structure of the universe. Infinitely small sub-atomic particles demand that highly advanced technology is stretched to its limit. The sense of wonder towards what complex phenomena these events may reveal is a fascination for many artists who are inevitably drawn to the laboratory.

At CERN, some of the most brilliant scientists of our time have shed light on the fundamental questions about our universe. By founding the first CERN Cultural Policy, the laboratory provided a specific means to reach other communities and to bring non-scientific voices into the research environment. The policy coincided with the founding of Arts at CERN in 2011, the official arts programme of the laboratory, which quickly became an influential platform dedicated to bringing science and art together in mutual inspiration. The vision of the programme was always beyond mere PR, having an awareness of bringing other viewpoints, perspectives and questions into the lab, a re-contextualisation of the practice of the scientists and an incentive for significant conversations between creative mindsets. Arts at CERN has evolved over the years, thanks to solid institutional support and a significant network of international collaborations, and is now running Collide, Accelerate and Guest Artists as annual schemes that bring artists into the laboratory from all over the world.

When the programme was founded, the goal was to stimulate discussion of the notion that science was not an isolated practice and interdisciplinarity was an essential part of creative research. CERN Director General Fabiola Gianotti stated in Davos this year that she is "very much in favour of a diverse and multidisciplinary culture, we have to break cultural silos, when people talk about the arts and humanities and science as if they were incompatible and mutually exclusive, but they are the highest expression of creativity, ingenuity, curiosity of humanity". Artists at CERN are welcomed as part of a strategy to open the lab to society and to invite creators to explore the challenges of imagining our world through other perspectives.

Artists working alongside scientists at CERN are encouraged to seek the limits of thinking in relation to the big questions of contemporary science. What are the conditions and the implications of artists working in this unique and complex research environment? What forms of creation take place in a highly specialized environment? What common grounds can be

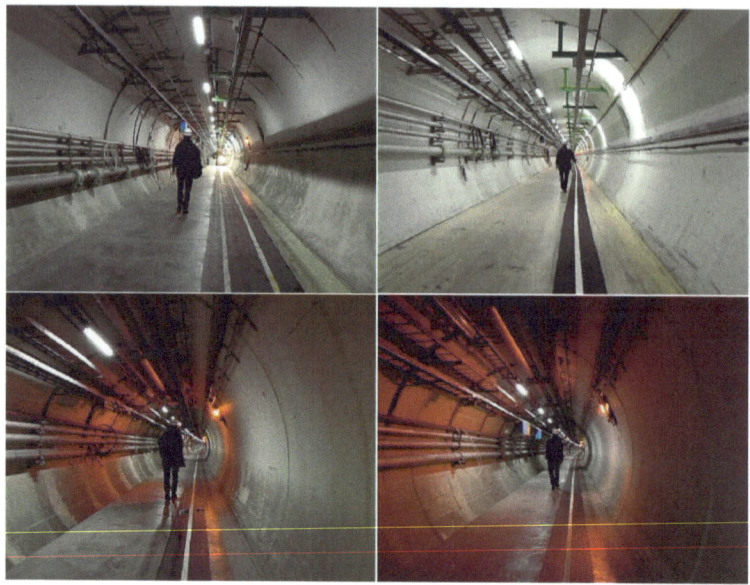

Artist Gianni Motti walks the 27 km underground ring at CERN.
Gianni Motti, *Walking for art's sake*, 2005
© 2005-2018 CERN

shared in order to negotiate the limits of contemporary creativity through different fields and experiences? How do methodologies of knowledge production connect with the big questions of our time?

Peter Jenni, former spokesperson for the ATLAS experiment, says, "Engaging with artists at CERN can enrich the personal motivation and satisfaction of working in the laboratory. Being challenged to have a broader view is ultimately beneficial." Experimental physicist Tamara Vázquez goes slightly further, saying that "the capability to step back and appreciate the research topic one is working on as part of a whole [creates] new paths to solve problems or new ways to interpret the results. This is precisely what working with artists does: it reminds us of the scale of the research we are doing and what we are ultimately trying to explain", thus bringing into focus the importance of cultural contextualisation and reflection that increasing numbers of scientists see as important for their own practice.

From a curatorial angle, Arts at CERN responds to a model of institutional cultural practice that nurtures and supports artists' engagement with contemporary science and fosters the research and production of deeply informed work. Artists are invited to confront and respond to an age of accelerating scientific and technological development and become active within the dynamics and complexities of the fundamental research environment. When artists arrive at CERN, the question of how we make sense of the experience of our world, and how the languages of art and science are applied to such questions, is a common and general motivation. That said, different people will of course bring different approaches, and the dynamics between individual artists and scientists always follow surprising paths.

The methodologies of advanced science and technology and its associated instruments situate the artist in an environment marked by a precision that is often unfamiliar to the arts. At CERN, a collective drive exists to set a common goal: uncovering the fundamental constituents of nature. The instruments developed for pursuing this goal take multiple forms and shapes, from discreet microcircuits to the vast scale of the Large Hadron Collider (LHC) and its detectors. On entering the lab, it becomes clear that it will not be straightforward to comprehend the broad range of experiments, their scale and function, and the models that represent deeply specialised mathematics. Today, science and technology play a crucial role in defining the human experience and understanding the tools and processes that enable knowledge to advance.

Without independent and radical thinkers in art and science, advances in knowledge would remain glacially slow. Furthermore, alongside independent thinkers we need pioneering ways of bringing together radical modes of thought and strategies for understanding. Physicist Mark Sutton suggests that "Increasingly our understanding of the world informs the way in which society functions, so it is important that we learn how to communicate the cutting edge of our understanding as widely and in as diverse a way as possible. Artistic engagement can help to keep that more in the forefront of our minds. It is another way in which we can keep connected with the real world". At CERN, artists make little attempt to depict the scientific concepts involved in their subject matter. Rather they reveal and explore phenomena, ideas and histories of discovery outside everyday human experience, making us able to sense and experience them or in some way grasp their significance and profoundness.

Phase Velocity & F-T-L in the G.V.D.
— *Jol Thomson*

The world's largest and most ancient freshwater lake, Lake Baikal in Siberia, is being partially transformed by the Russian Institute for Nuclear Research into a cubic kilometre scale neutrino telescope. In 2017, I was invited to join and document the processes of this rift lake being instrumented with optical devices meant to capture the strange inferences of the most abundant and most elusive particle in the universe, the neutrino fermion. We can never directly perceive a neutrino. We can only infer it by its weak-interactions with our electromagnetic or baryonic matter (the stuff that makes up the 4 per cent of matter and energy we actually know anything about). The arrayed optical modules that the scientists and engineers sink into the lake (that holds 30 per cent of the entire worlds melted freshwater), operate to detect a fascinating event that deeply captures my imagination: superluminality.

Most people take for granted the idea that "nothing can travel faster than light". So engrained in our minds is this belief, so fundamental, that we must have learned not to question it. When I tell people that the statement is not entirely accurate, or rather that it is only accurate in a very specific context - one to which we do not usually have access - most do not immediately believe me. It is however with these sorts of cognitive anomalies or dissonances that we may begin to wonder what other inaccuracies we hold in our day to day lives?

There are billions of neutrinos passing through you and me at every instant, and from all directions. Physicists say that neutrinos could pass through 100 light years of lead without slowing. These strange leptons are a radical imperceptible other. I like to think of these anarchic neutral miniscules as my 'flavourful' collaborators.[1] The only way we can detect or infer their existence, and begin to unpack the weird ontology of these strange entities, is through the detection of faster-than-light (FTL) signals that occur when they collide with or cascade into our type of 'regular' baryonic matter.

We only infer neutrinos because of an ultraviolet radiation called Cherenkov radiation. This superluminal blue occurs when something travels faster than light in a given medium, like gas-atmosphere, or liquid-water (or solid water for that matter). This phenomenon is why nuclear fission reactors glow blue. They're emitting bundles of FTL particles in the heavy water meant to control the fission processes. The 'phase velocity of light' is different across mediums, and the usual epithet is missing in the statement, "nothing travels faster than light in the vacuum of space". Here in our dense atmosphere, on our ocean-wet planet,

---

1 Physicists refer to flavours of neutrinos based on their differing and determining energy masses. Each of the three flavors has a slightly different mass. Strangely enough, and unlike any other known or measured particle, neutrinos change their flavour while travelling.

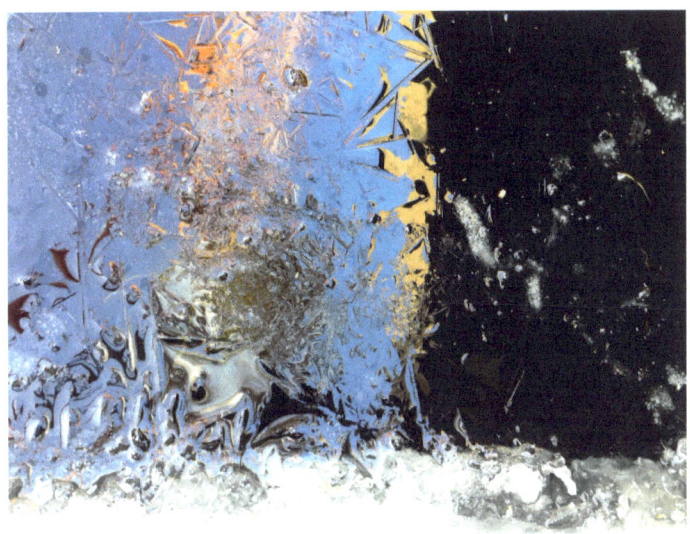

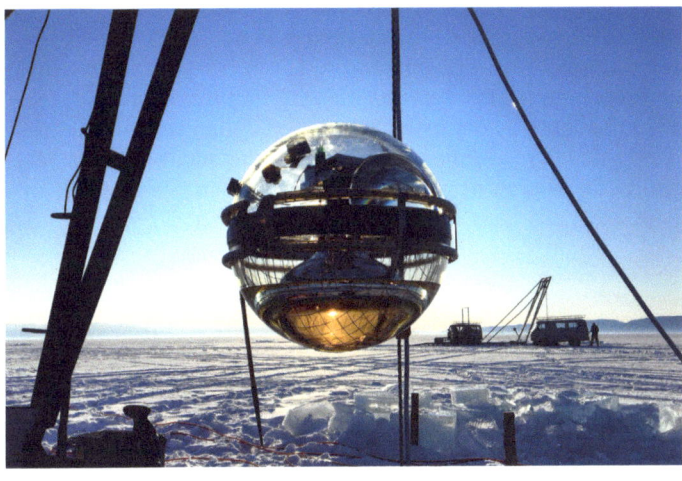

GVD, Lake Baikal, Siberia, Russia.
Photos: Jol Thomson

the speed of light is a third less than it is in space. Neutrino decay in our baryonic charged matter causes particles to travel faster than photons can in these mediums, leaving the tell-tale superluminal blues. That's why so many physicists across the planet are developing very large-scale detector-assemblages with and within vast 'laboratory-landscapes'.

The 'Gigaton Volume Detector'(GVD) at Lake Baikal performs as a posthuman sensory assemblage becoming an Earthly, elemental form. Technology becomes planetary body and, amongst other things, this transmutation complicates traditional longstanding binaries between, for example, technology and nature. Human and non-human relationships between landscape, technology, elements, and the cosmos explicitly coalesce at these sites into palpable philosophical engagements with scale, ecology, agency, and even ethics. A handful of feminist science studies scholars refer to the physics-philosophy implicitly at play here as the 'quantum reformulation of ontology'.

Some of our most basic presuppositions about life, the universe and everything are, if not wrong, usually specific to a given context which is rarely articulated. The specificity of a law or rule, the context within which it might be or is usually valid, often goes unspoken and unaccounted for. The term 'phase velocity of light' refers to the fact that light has different speed limits, and therefore, things like sub-atomic particles can and do move faster than light.

One of my main motivations to work with/in physics lies in unpacking these anomalies (and others like them) as triggers for thought, as challenges to our conceptions, our understandings, our traditions. I work with my collaborators and their complex sites of detection (themselves fantastic and challenging) to extend criticisms about what it is we think we know and how and to whom we think we ought to address this knowledge. This is where posthumanism and the decentering of human exceptionalism comes into play.

If we look at the state of the planet Earth in the 21st century, it should be pretty clear that we need radically to re-learn, unlearn, and even risk our traditional conceptions/beliefs/principles/ desires. As the recently departed Ursula K. Le Guin wrote in *Arts of Living on a Damaged Planet*, "Changing our minds is going to be a big change. To use the world well, to be able to stop wasting it and our time in it, we need to relearn our being in it".

References

Tsing, A. L., Bubandt, N., Gan, E., & Swanson, H. A. (2017). Arts of Living on a *Damaged Planet: Ghosts and Monsters of the Anthropocene*. University of Minnesota Press.

A Synthetic Universe — Blanca Pujals

Over the last decades, new architectures and infrastructures for containing and artificially reproducing the conditions at the very beginning of the universe have surfaced across the world.

A synthetic replica of the early universe on Earth.

These sophisticated technospaces are sealed chambers that recreate specific and inexistent physical conditions on Earth to reveal the origin of matter. They spread throughout a subterranean global chamber system:

an invisible underground network.

After the nuclear fission era and the cold war, the sub-atomic particle époque is created by a new configuration of alliances. New forms of energy and knowledge are creating new forms of political and scientific alliances.

New supranational laboratories like CERN transformed physics into a force within politics, creating new spaces of negotiation and agreement. Subatomic particles question the Standard Model of Particle Physics while scientific infrastructures challenge previous models of political alliances and social structures.

The tiny monastic laboratory of the seventeenth century has been replaced by a global technoscientific infrastructure spread across the world. The elementary particle physics infrastructures involve massive urban complexes, buildings, and chambers, designed to host the invisible. They are comprised of scientists, particles, liquids, data, politics and technologies working together for the production of knowledge.

The invisible underground network of elementary particle infrastructures around the world is a sensing architecture, which amplifies new political and material interactions. Maybe we can say that every new scientific experimental chamber is the architect of a new époque of hybrid systems of transnational and transhuman collaborations.

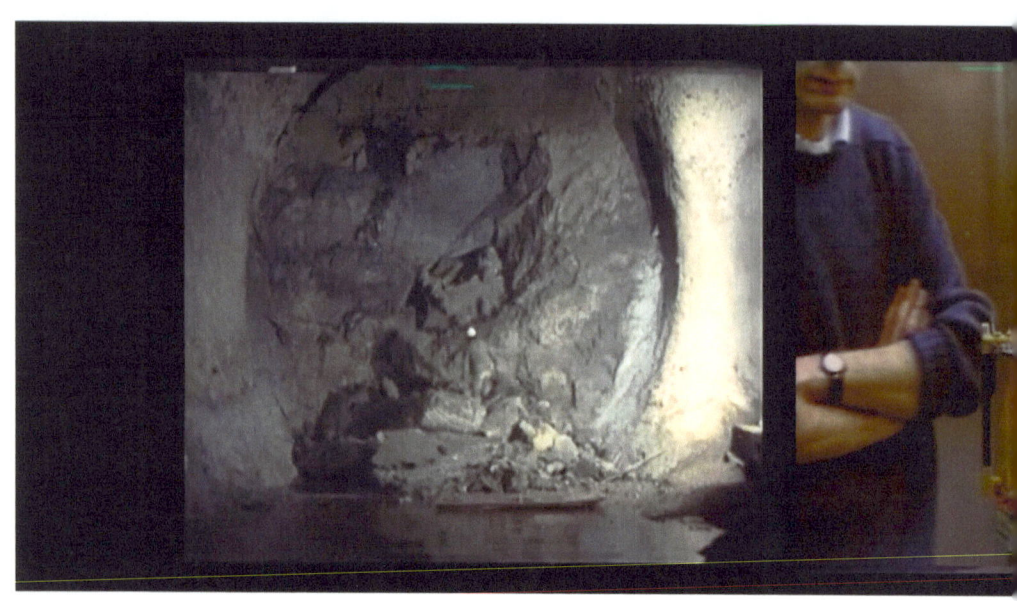

Blanca Pujals. *A Synthetic Universe. The Unmaking of Microscopic
Bonds in Transnational Space*, 2016. Three-channel video installation.
Colour. Stereo. HDV. 18'44''. (Images from CERN's historical archive).

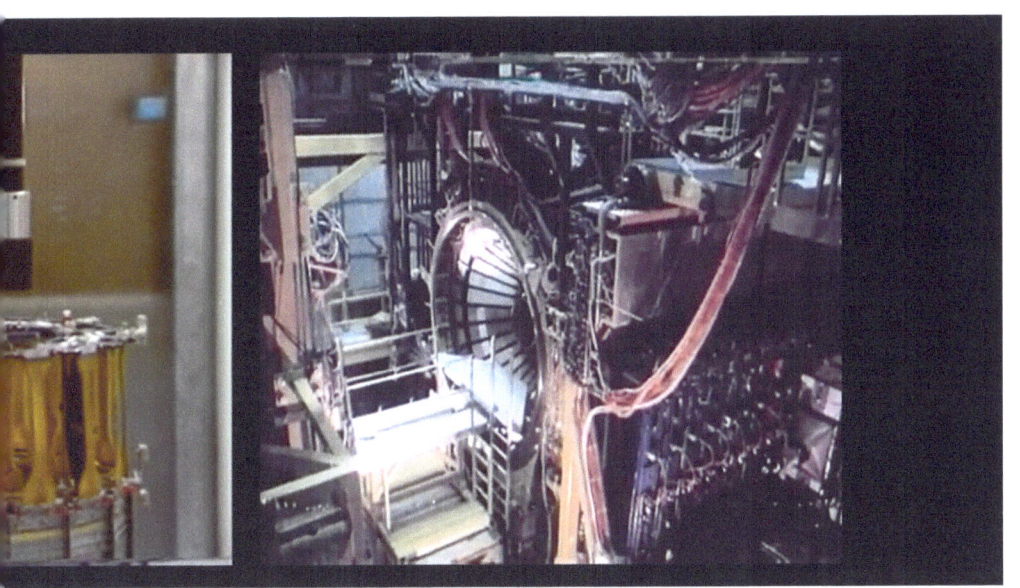

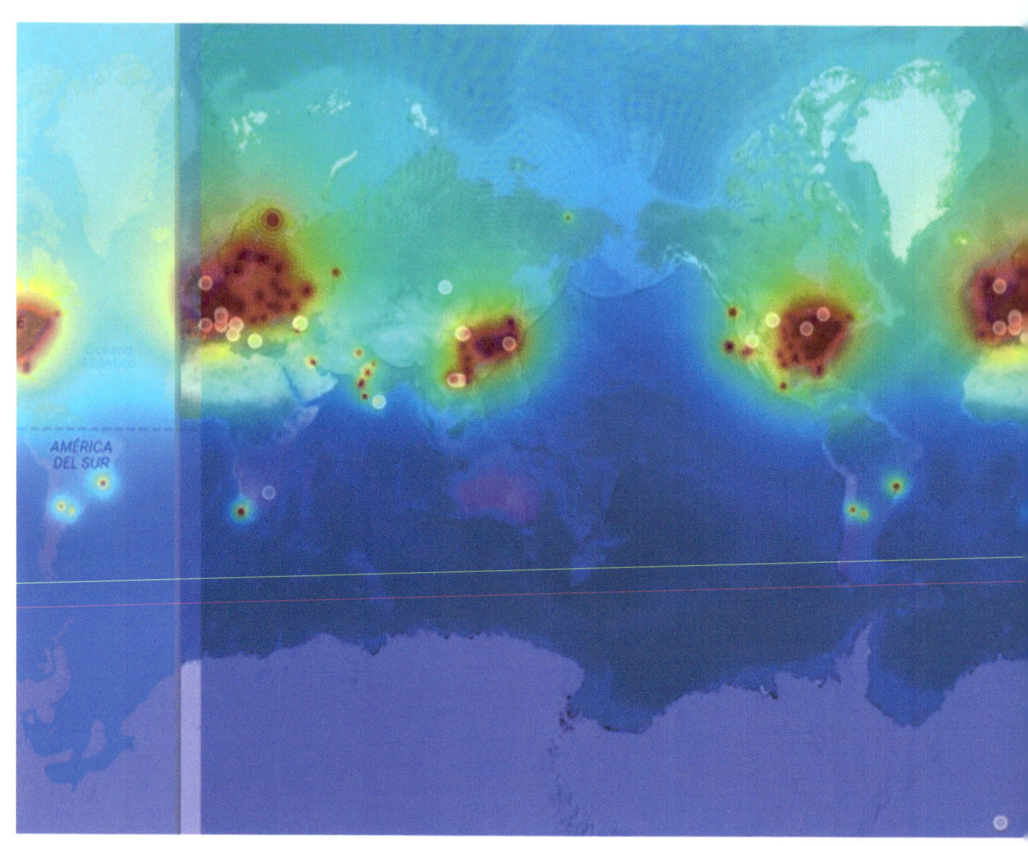

Blanca Pujals. *A Synthetic Universe. The Unmaking of Microscopic Bonds in Transnational Space*, 2016. This map is part of the GoogleMap archive made for the project. It shows the elementary particle colliders and neutrino observatories and architectures (GoogleMap, Blanca Pujals, 2016) merged with the Synthetic Antineutrino Global Map 2015 that shows the human-made synthetic antineutrinos emissions from nuclear test sites and nuclear power plants. The Antineutrino Global Map was created in 2015 with data from two neutrino detectors: Borexino (Italy) and Kamiokande (Japan). This was combined with data from the International Atomic Energy Agency on more than 400 operational nuclear reactors. Merging these two maps, we can visualise the relationship between two different nuclear periods: fission-fusion and elemental particles. Moreover, it allows consideration of geopolitical relationships in relation to the scientific experimental knowledge and the scientific structures produced by neutrino and the study of the elemental particles of the universe.

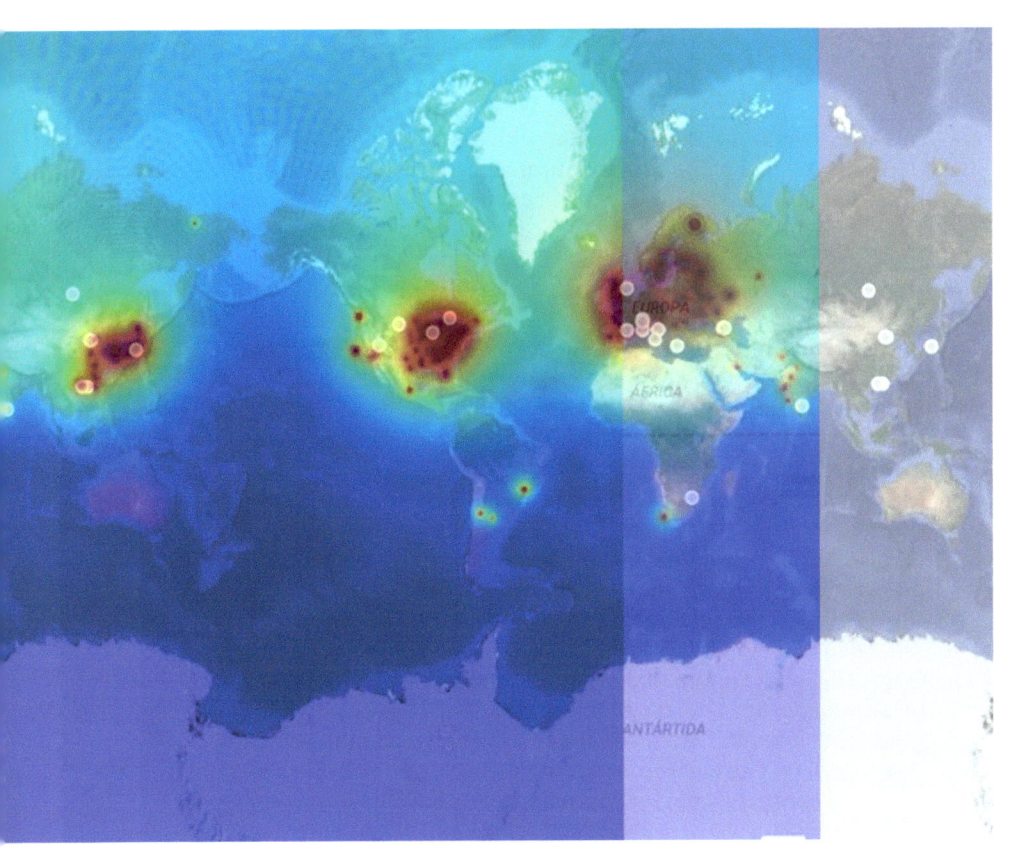

Contributors' biographies

Mónica Bello is a Spanish curator with over 10 years' experience in designing and managing artistic programs in pioneering interdisciplinary institutions in Europe. Since March 2015, she has been the Head of Arts at CERN at the European Organization for Nuclear Research in Geneva. Prior to that, she was the Artistic Director of VIDA (2010 - 2015), the International Award organised by Fundación Telefónica, Madrid (Spain). From 2008 to 2010, she initiated and ran the Department of Education at Laboral Centro de Arte, Gijón(Spain). Later, she was a member of the Board of Trustees of Fundación Laboral Centro de Arte. She is co-founder of Capsula, a curatorial platform on art, science and nature.

Ansuman Biswas was born in Calcutta and trained in the UK. He is an artist with an international practice encompassing music, film, live art, installation, writing and theatre. In 2002-2003, he was artist-in-residence at the National Institute of Medical Research. He has an ongoing research interest in consciousness studies. Ansuman has shown visual and time-based art at Tate Modern, South London Gallery, Whitechapel Gallery, the Institute of Contemporary Arts, London, IIC New Delhi, Headlands Centre, San Francisco, and many other galleries and museums around the world. He has worked as a composer and musician in a wide range of contexts from jazz to Indian classical music, pop songs to industrial noise.

Annie Carpenter is an artist whose practice addresses links between science and the labour of artists, through exposing the process of 'working'. Themes of trying, failing and industry are recurrent and are explored through sculpture, video, curating, and writing. In October 2015, she embarked on an international art/science expedition to Svalbard through Arctic Circle, New York. Annie curated the 2013 series of curated exhibitions *Free Failing* at Rogue Project Space alongside Taneesha Ahmed. She is the founder and coordinator of Art & Science Critical Forum in Manchester and gained a BSc (Hons) in Natural Sciences, specialising in Astronomy and Planetary Science.

Dr Flaviu Cipcigan is a physicist at IBM Research UK and one of Forbes '30 under 30'. He is working at the interface between data, physics and biology, designing new antibiotics via computer simulation and AI. His PhD from the University of Edinburgh on computer modelling of molecules has been recognised by the Institute of Physics as a "leading contribution in advancing theoretical condensed matter physics". He is also a dancer, with a background in Argentine tango and bachata, and a graphic designer. His art pieces, created in collaboration with artists, include *Unstable Structures*, exploring representations of scientific knowledge, and *Markov*, where mathematical models are used for new styles of musical minimalism.

Phil Coy is an artist. He often works with architects, software developers, and scientists to make films and public works that explore the intersection between digital and analogue representation. His work collages concepts rooted in the radical art and literature of the 20th century with the languages and architectures of contemporary global commerce. Forthcoming / recent exhibitions / screenings include: Annely Juda Fine Art (2018); South London Gallery (2018); Royal Observatory Greenwich (2018); York Museum and Art Gallery (2018-19); FACT (2017); Ferens Art Gallery and Hull Maritime Museum (2017); Wilkinson Gallery (2016); 58th and 59th BFI London Film Festivals (2014 and 2015).

Fiona Crisp is Professor of Fine Art at Northumbria University, Newcastle where she leads the research group *The Cultural Negotiation of Science*. Her recent Leverhulme-funded Fellowship, *Material Sight*, uses non-documentary photography and moving image to interrogate extremes of visual and imaginative representation in fundamental science and technology, foregrounding the laboratory as a social, cultural, and political space where meaning is shaped and constructed rather than received or observed. Crisp's work is represented by Matt's Gallery London and is held in several national permanent collections including Tate, the British Council, Arts Council and the Government Art Collection.

Dr Chamkaur Ghag is a Reader and the Dark Matter group leader in the Department of Physics and Astronomy at University College London (UCL). Chamkaur has been working in the field of Dark Matter for 14 years, operating rare-event search experiments in deep underground laboratories in search of Dark Matter signals. Ghag is Chair of the Dark Matter UK, the UK Principal Investigator for the LUX Dark Matter experiment, a member of the LUX-ZEPLIN (LZ) experiment. He is also Principal Investigator for the Boulby Underground Germanium Suite (BUGS) and manages the Radon Facility at Rutherford Appleton Laboratory. He is Chair of the Science and Technology Facilities Council (STFC)'s Particle Astrophysics Advisory Panel.

Dr Marek Kukula is the Public Astronomer, Royal Observatory Greenwich. Marek obtained his PhD in Radio Astronomy at Jodrell Bank Observatory, then carried out research into distant galaxies and supermassive black holes at several institutions including the University of Edinburgh and the Space Telescope Science Institute. Marek is a judge on the Insight Astronomy Photographer of the Year competition and was curator of *Visions of the Universe*, a major exhibition on the history of astrophotography. Marek is the author of *The Intimate Universe* and the co-author of *The Scientific Secrets of Doctor Who*, both published in 2015.

Harry Lawson is an artist, living and working in London. Recent solo exhibitions include *Walking with a Ghost*, Southard Reid (2017), *Cave*, Kingsgate Workshops, London, (2017); *Remote Future, Remote Past*, Apartment Projects, London (2014). Group shows include *Uncommon Chemistry*, Observer Building, Hastings (2016) and *Absolute Dating*, One Thoresby Street, Nottingham (2015). He graduated with an MA in Sculpture from the Royal College of Art, London (2013).

Dr Massimo Mannarelli is coordinator of the Theory Group at Laboratori Nazionali del Gran Sasso, Italy. Massimo obtained his PhD in Physics at the University of Bari and has held postdocs in US, at the Texas A&M University and at the MIT, and then in Barcelona at the UAB and UB. He has worked on several aspects of theoretical physics, including applications of quantum chromodynamics to compact stars and heavy ion collisions. He is interested in approaching unsolved problems in physics by developing new theoretical methods and strategies.

Nahum is an artist and musician based in Berlin. His work focuses on producing projects that explore the possibilities of generating wonder and enchantment. By using outer space technologies and illusionism methods, his work creates extreme perspectives that address unconventional human experiences. In 2014, Nahum was recognised as a Young Space Leader by the International Astronautical Federation for his cultural contributions to outer space activities. He is a graduate of the International Space University. He is also the Founding Director of KOSMICA, a global institute devoted to developing critical and poetic projects about outer space activities and their impact on Earth.

Dr Mark Neyrinck studies the arrangement of matter and galaxies in the universe, called the cosmic web. He has worked on a correspondence of artistic interest: the geometry of the cosmic web is shared by both origami tessellations, and structural-engineering spiderwebs such as dreamcatchers. He is fascinated by all sorts of visualisations, sonifications, and tactilisations of scientific concepts and data. His PhD is from the University of Colorado at Boulder, and he has held postdoc positions at the University of Hawaii, Johns Hopkins University, and the Institute for Computational Cosmology in Durham.

Blanca Pujals is an architect, artist and writer whose work examines the material conditions of representation through a wide approach to the idea of architecture. She got her BA in Architecture at Barcelona School of Architecture. She completed her studies with a MA in Critical Theory and Museum Studies at the Independent Studies Program of MACBA Museum. She was recently a postgraduate at the Centre for Research Architecture (Visual Cultures) at Goldsmiths University of London, where she received a distinction. Her practice is based on spatial research and critical analysis. Her work encompasses film, architecture, curatorial projects as well as lectures and different displays of writing.

Tomás Saraceno is an Argentinian artist based in Berlin. He takes inspiration in the adaptability, integrity, and beauty of such natural formations as molecular chains, clouds, and spider webs. He creates drawings, sculptures, and site specific installations that apply these natural structures to the problem of developing alternative constructions for living that would enable humans to more responsively and responsibly inhabit the planet. His work has been exhibited at The Metropolitan Museum of Art; Grand Palais, Paris; NTU Centre for Contemporary Art Singapore; and many other venues around the world. The artist has participated in the International Space Studies Program at NASA's Ames Research Center and held residencies at Centre National d'Études Spatiales in Paris and MIT's Center for Art, Science & Technology. In 2009, he presented a major installation at the 53rd Venice Biennale and was awarded the prestigious Calder Prize.

Dr Suchitra Sebastian holds an MS and PhD in Applied Physics from Stanford University, and an MBA from the Indian Institute of Management (Ahmedabad). She is currently University Reader in Physics at the University of Cambridge. Suchitra was recently named as one of thirty 'Exceptional Young Scientists' by the World Economic Forum and one of the top ten 'Next big names in Physics' by the Financial Times. She is the recipient of a L'Oreal-UNESCO fellowship for women in science, among other awards.

Semiconductor are artist duo, Ruth Jarman and Joe Gerhardt. In their art works, they explore the material nature of our world and how we experience it through the lens of science and technology. They have been awarded numerous honours and grants including the Samsung Art + Prize for New Media, a Smithsonian Artist Research Fellowship, a NASA Space Sciences Fellowship and a Jerwood Open Forest commission. They have exhibited and screened their works at the House of Electronic Arts Basel, FACT Liverpool, ArtScience Museum Singapore, San Francisco Museum of Modern Art, Royal Academy of Arts London, the Sundance Film Festival Utah and at the International Film Festival Rotterdam.

Professor Tara Shears is an experimental particle physicist and Professor of Physics at the University of Liverpool. Her research focuses on testing the limits of our understanding of particle physics, using data collected by the LHCb experiment, one of seven particle physics detector experiments at CERN's Large Hadron Collider (LHCb stands for Large Hadron Collider beauty). She is interested in understanding why that there is so little antimatter in the universe, where and how our current understanding breaks down, and what lies beyond it. She is also interested in how some of the unseen, non-intuitive aspects of physics can be experienced and visualised, and how art can provide a different, illuminating angle.

Tavares Strachan is a Bahamian artist based in New York, whose work explores aspects of science, art, and the environment to create works that are ambitious in scale and scope. Many of his projects investigate the nature of invisibility, calling into question the conditions that frame and legitimize certain cultural knowledge and histories while obscuring and erasing others. His experience at the Russian Cosmonaut Training Center in Star City and skill as a master diver have both played a role in his art. His focus on absence and presence led him to stage *Seen/Unseen* in 2011, an exhibition of work in an undisclosed location never open to the public. In 2013, Strachan represented the Bahamas at the 55th Venice Biennale.

Jol Thomson is an interdisciplinary artist and researcher producing film installations with weak force particle detectors, including the IceCube Neutrino Observatory, the Gigaton Volume Detector in Siberia, The Laboratori Nazionali del Gran Sasso, and others. In 2017 he was awarded a doctoral studentship and has begun a practice based PhD in Arts and Sciences at the University of Westminster, London. Before joining the Westminster, he was awarded the MERU Art*Science Award for his film $G24|0v\beta\beta$, was a fellow at Akademie Schloss Solitude, Stuttgart, a scientific researcher at the Technical University of Braunschweig, Berlin, and received training at the Städelschule in Frankfurt aM.

Dr Nicola Triscott is a cultural producer, curator, writer and researcher, specialising in the intersections between art, science, technology and society. She is founder and Artistic Director/CEO of Arts Catalyst, and Principal Research Fellow in Transdisciplinary Art and Science at the University of Westminster. She has built Arts Catalyst, which she founded in 1994, into one of the UK's most distinctive arts organisations, distinguished by its international projects and ambitious artists' commissions that engage with science. Nicola lectures and publishes internationally. She has edited books on art and technology in the Arctic, art and space, the art and cetacean encounters of Ariel Guzik, and ecological art. She has a PhD in Curatorial Studies from the University of Westminster.

Credits

The Live Creature and Ethereal Things: Physics in Culture is published by Arts Catalyst. Supported by The Leverhulme Trust and the Science and Technology Facilities Council.

This book captures conversations initiated between artists, physicists and curators at an experimental workshop held at the Institute of Physics, London in October 2017. It is published to accompany the exhibition *Material Sight* by Fiona Crisp at Arts Catalyst, 7 June - 14 July 2018. The exhibition was also shown at the Northern Gallery for Contemporary Art, 24 March – 13 May 2018.

Research for the book has been supported by The Leverhulme Trust, Northumbria University Newcastle, University of Westminster and Arts Catalyst.

Thanks to all the book contributors, Boulby Underground Laboratory, Durham University Institute of Computational Cosmology, Laboratori Nazionali del Gran Sasso, Arts Catalyst team, and the Institute of Physics.

www.artscatalyst.org
www.materialsight.wordpress.com

Arts Catalyst
74-76 Cromer Street
London WC1H 8DR

Designed by Rita Peres Pereira

ISBN 978-0-9927776-4-7

**ARTS
CATALYST**

LEVERHULME
TRUST _____

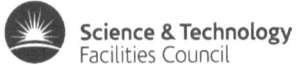
Science & Technology
Facilities Council